HOLIDAYS IN

RETIREMENT

Holidays in Retirement

A GUIDE TO TRIPS AROUND EUROPE

JOSEPH SMITH

foulsham

LONDON • NEW YORK • TORONTO • SYDNEY

foulsham

The Publishing House, Bennetts Close,
Cippenham, Berkshire SL1 5AP England

ISBN 0-572-02150-X

Typeset in Great Britain by Typesetting Solutions, Slough, Berks.
Printed in Great Britain

for

Rosemary

Ideal companion in Europe as in Life

Acknowledgements

I must record my appreciation of the vital part in the preparation of this book played by my son, Ambrose, and his wife, Judith, who transformed much of my crude typescript into beautiful word-processed perfection. My granddaughter, Rosemary Jane Cowley, and my former secretary, Julie Ingham, also contributed to this process.

I have to thank the rest of my family for their encouragement and frequently their forebearance during the period of the book's preparation. Nor must I forget to thank my friend Andrew Duncan, mentioned in Chapter Eight on Portugal, whose constant prodding helped significantly to overcome my initial inertia.

Chapter Eleven on Sicily and Southern Italy, would never have been written without the generous offer of my friend Eric Wolstenholme to accompany me on that trip.

Most of the tours described in Part Two were organised for me with unfailing efficiency by Frances Liddiard, press officer of Saga Holidays, to whom I am extremely grateful.

Finally, I am deeply indebted to my literary agent, Jeffrey Simmons, without whose expert knowledge of the publishing world the book would certainly never have seen the light of day.

JOSEPH SMITH

CONTENTS

Prologue

Writers generally seem to find it useful and appropriate to preface their books with an introduction. Hilaire Belloc, for instance, in his travel classic, *The Path to Rome,* wrote an introduction called simply 'Praise of this Book'. I, too, feel that an introduction to this book is desirable, not indeed to praise it, but rather to explain how it claims to be a travel book with a difference.

Part One of the book is an account of the tremendous enjoyment that two active pensioners have discovered in the new opportunities that retirement has provided to wander by car, just as the spirit moved them, around those parts of Europe that they had always wanted to explore. Part Two is complementary to this, and describes the equally rewarding experiences of more organised expeditions to parts of Europe further afield under the expert guidance of Saga Holidays, the leading specialists in travel for the over-60s.

The book therefore seeks primarily to interest those fortunate people who are already enjoying the well-earned rewards of their long years of work, and are now embarked on a happy, active retirement. It hopes to encourage them to use their new-found leisure constructively to sample the wonderfully varied delights, scenic, cultural, historical, religious and gastronomic of our European heritage. Equally, the book hopes to be of considerable interest to those still earning their daily bread, but who are beginning to look forward with growing anticipation to the liberation that will come with the years of retirement now gradually appearing on the horizon.

The interest of my wife and myself in European travel was first awakened in our student days at university. There Rosemary was fortunate enough to study European and medieval history under such famous historians as Namier, Jacob and A.J.P. Taylor. She wrote a highly praised thesis on the bizarre activities of one Hartang von Kluck. This gentleman, who later became something of a family joke, was some sort of fifteenth century under-cover agent, a kind of medieval James Bond. Rosemary had traced his sinister movements round the courts of Europe, but only from manuscripts unearthed in libraries. She hoped one day to follow his movements on the ground.

My own European interests went back rather further. My classics degree included ancient history and classical archaeology. I did indeed visit Rome with a school party before the war. But my juvenile appreciation of 'The Grandeur That Was Rome' was hopelessly distorted by the propaganda of a modern pseudo-Caesar, Benito Mussolini. As for 'The Glory That Was Greece', the nearest I got to that was a day trip to the British Museum to see the Elgin Marbles.

Thereafter our lives seemed to get ever busier both domestically and professionally. We did manage a memorable silver wedding celebration to the cities of northern Italy. But our big breakthrough into Europe did not finally occur till the decade before our retirement, when we chanced to hit upon the device of exchanging our house for the summer holidays with families abroad. This gave us a fascinating insight into family life in Holland, Sweden, Germany and Italy, as well as opportunities to tour large parts of those countries in some depth.

These exchange holidays served to whet our appetite for the more thorough exploration of Europe that we had promised ourselves when retirement at last provided the opportunity. When the great day arrived, we lost no time at all and were off on R + 1 for a month's tour of northern Italy. In the years that followed, we made similar long tours by car of France, Spain and Italy. The most notable of these I describe in Part One.

Although tremendously stimulating and enjoyable, these independent journeys, we had to admit, were becoming gradually more exhausting. And we still had not been to Greece! We studied the maps and were frankly intimidated. The journey by car would involve the best part of England, France and Italy plus two ferry crossings, before we could even begin the holiday. We decided, albeit with considerable misgivings, to settle for the obvious alternative, a package tour.

We examined the brochures. It was quickly clear that Saga's 'Tour of Classical Greece' offered precisely what we were looking for. In the event we enjoyed not only the visits to all the famous historical sites, but also the luxurious hotels, the well-planned itinerary and, above all, the congenial company of like-minded veterans. So began a continuing love affair with Saga Holidays. Further trips followed in quick succession to Andalucia, Portugal, Italy, Poland, Madeira, Yugoslavia, Sicily and southern Italy. I describe the best of our adventures in Part Two.

In these various ways we achieved our ambition to explore Europe thoroughly in our retirement. Gradually, in parallel with all this, there developed a related interest that we had not particularly planned. Friends asked me so many questions about our early house exchange holidays that it occurred to me that it might be a good idea to write something about them. So one day I dashed off an article and sent it to the *Guardian* newspaper. To my pleasant surprise it appeared almost immediately in a series called 'Easing the Squeeze'. The country was apparently suffering one of its periodic recessions, and by sheer chance the piece was just right.

To my even greater surprise, the series then won some journalistic award, and I was invited to the presentation celebration in London. As a journalist with just one solitary article to his credit, I modestly declined the invitation. However, when we began our retirement travels, I wondered whether the media might be similarly interested. I soon found that the 'quality' press such as *The Observer* and *The Daily Telegraph* were ready to accept my occasional travel articles. In particular, *The Universe*, the Catholic weekly, which at that time had a large and highly regarded travel section, commissioned a whole series of articles from me.

The pleasant surprises continued when we began our Saga trips. For example, *Choice Magazine* printed a beautifully illustrated account of our first Saga holiday to Greece, though with the slightly unfortunate title, 'Making a Package of the Parthenon'. The culmination of this catalogue of pleasant surprises was when Saga Holidays generously invited us to be their guests on future expeditions as a sort of 'quid pro quo'.

Now friends have persuaded me that the history of our travels should be put into the permanent form of a book. So here it is! But there I must stop lest I should be in danger of emulating Belloc's 'Praise of This Book'.

PART ONE

Europe by car

CHAPTER ONE

France–Provence

We have enjoyed tremendously our tours by car in several European countries, but France is definitely our favourite. There are two very practical considerations which add to the motorist's enjoyment of the infinitely varied tourist attractions of this beautiful country. The first is the French system of minor roads. These, marked as 'D' roads on the map, stretch in an intricate network over almost the whole country, and provide a very satisfactory alternative to the busy motorways and 'routes nationales'. In many areas these minor roads, which are generally well maintained, will be completely deserted for mile after mile, with the occasional farm tractor the only traffic hazard.

The second and even more important fact is that in many villages along these minor roads, and frequently elsewhere as well, one can discover small country hotels which are quite remarkable value for money. The mod. cons. may sometimes be minimal, but the meals will generally be magnificent. I could quote dozens of these delightful discoveries. One that stands out in our memory was a tiny wayside hotel in the gorge of the River Tarn. The proprietor, a little old lady, brought in a succession of marvellous dishes with a twinkle in her eye, and seemed to be saying 'Just see what I've got for you now!' And the bill in the morning was so ridiculously small that we felt morally obliged to give her an outsize reward as 'service'.

Friends who have read my newspaper articles on different parts of France, often ask which area I would most strongly recommend for their next holiday. It's a terribly difficult question to answer from the *embarras de richesse* that France has to offer. One would think first, perhaps, of the valleys of the Loire and the Dordogne with their magnificent historic chateaux. Or perhaps of those other wonderfully scenic valleys, the Tarn, the Lot and the Ardèche. Other strong competitors are the captivating 'villages fleuris' of Alsace and the stunning mountain scenery of the Juras and the Pyrenees.

Finally, however, we would have to settle for the infinitely varied attractions, scenic, historic and gastronomic, of Provence. Because of its perfect climate, and particularly its mild winters, Provence, and especially its coastline 'The Riviera', was the favourite holiday resort of the rich and famous before air travel allowed the Spanish Costas to compete. The beaches, of course, are still popular with sun worshippers. For us, however, the main attractions are well inland, where, for instance, some of the finest Roman remains outside Italy are to be found. This is only to be expected, since the very name 'Provence' comes from the Latin *provincia*, and the region was the first, and for some time the only, Roman province outside Italy.

The most celebrated Roman remains are the arenas of Arles and Nîmes, the Theatre of Orange, and the much-photographed Pont du Gard. Both arenas can accommodate on their terraces over 20,000 spectators and are still in use, though sadly, mainly for bull-fights. Nîmes also possesses one of the most beautiful small temples of the ancient world, the curiously named Maison Carrée, which is a slender architectural gem.

Far and away the most impressive of these Roman antiquities is the Theatre of Orange. Quite staggeringly huge, it is also astonishingly well-preserved, especially its enormous stage wall, 103 metres long and 38 metres high, which Louis XIV called 'the most remarkable wall in my kingdom'. In a niche, high up on this wall, there still stands, quite unbelievably, the original, albeit restored, statue of the Emperor Augustus.

We noted with pleasure that in the high season this fine old theatre was still being put to good use with performances of Verdi operas and even his *Requiem*, while for other tastes there was jazz with Benny Goodman and Stephane Grappelli. Not far from the theatre, standing on a traffic island in the middle of the road to Montelimar, is Orange's other major monument, the great Triumphal Arch, erected after Julius Caesar's victories in 49 BC and the third largest of its kind in the Roman world.

Our own favourite Roman antiquities we found in none of these famous places, but rather in the little-known town of Vaison la Romaine. Here, probably better than anywhere, apart from Pompeii and Herculaneum, one gets a vivid impression of the life-style of wealthy Romans of the early Empire. Twelve acres of excavations have revealed a series of desirable residences, complete even with under-floor central heating, a technique later forgotten for about 1,500 years! There is also a small Roman theatre and a bridge still capable of sustaining the traffic of the twentieth century.

Vaison is not simply all 'La Romaine', however; it is nowadays a pleasant little holiday resort, while across that Roman bridge, on a steep hillside, is a beautifully intact medieval village. This, neglected and largely deserted for many years, has recently been brought back to life, and its lovely old buildings restored.

The magnificent countryside around Vaison la Romaine is dominated by the massive Mont Ventoux, an isolated outcrop of the Alps. The mountain is more than twice the height of Scafell Pike, but nevertheless has a perfectly manageable road to the top. Provided that you don't mind innumerable hair-pin bends, the gradients are not particularly difficult until the last couple of hundred yards or so, when the surface is a bit dodgy.

Needless to say, the view from the top is ample reward, although the mountain fully lives up to its name of 'Mount Windy'. On the far horizon is the whole panorama of the snow-capped Alps with the centrepiece the gleaming white of the Mont Blanc massif. Mont Ventoux has also given its name to one of the most notable wines of Provence. It is yet another amenity of Vaison la Romaine that there is a most convenient *cave* sharing a building with the Tourist Information Office right in the centre of the town. *Dégustations* of the local wine are readily available.

Avignon, of course, featured in one of the darkest periods of the history of the Church, when Pope Clement V was forced to abandon Rome and take refuge in France. Altogether seven Popes resided there until 1377, when Gregory XI, stung by the reproaches of that remarkable woman, St Catherine of Siena, plucked up his courage and returned to Rome.

The massive palace of the Popes still stands as a reminder of those troubled times. Sombre and fortress-like, rather than palatial, it is now the scene of Avignon's summer festival of music and drama. Not far from the Palais des Papes is the celebrated Pont St Bénézet which ends rather dramatically halfway across the Rhône. Everyone has heard of the famous song 'Sur le pont d'Avignon, on y danse, on y danse'. However, those tiresome historical researchers appear to have proved conclusively that *sur* is a corruption of *sous*, and that the revels actually took place on the bank beneath not on the bridge. Is nothing sacred?

There is an ancient tradition, firmly held by the French, that in the very early days of the Church, a group of Christ's closest disciples were driven by persecution from the Holy Land and arrived as refugees in the south of France. We had encountered this tradition already at Rocamadour in the Dordogne, where the view across a deep gorge of Rocamadour clinging most improbably to its cliff-face is quite breathtaking. According to this ancient tradition, Zacchae'us, the diminutive disciple, who was frustrated because his view of Jesus was blocked by taller men in front of him, and who climbed a sycamore tree to get a better view (Luke 19, 1-10), was one of these refugees and lived as a hermit in a cave on the rock-face at Rocamadour.

As a result, Rocamadour claims to be the oldest centre of pilgrimage in France. A medieval document states that at Easter 1403, a boatman helped 3,918 pilgrims to cross the River Dordogne on their way to Rocamadour. However, my medieval historian wife pointed out that these pilgrims almost certainly would be on their way across France to make the much more famous pilgrimage to Santiago de Compostela in Spain, and would be taking in Rocamadour en route.

On another exploration of the valley of the River Lot, we found a very similar situation with the Abbey of Conques, which also became immensely rich and famous as a convenient resting place on another route across France for pilgrims to Compostela. But more, much more, about that later.

Coming back to Provence, we find the most notable example of the tradition in the little town of Saintes Maries de la Mer on the coast of the Camargue, that strange region of lagoons, wild horses, pink flamingoes and fighting bulls in the estuary of the River Rhône. According to this version of the story, Mary Jacobé and Mary Salomé who, with their vase of perfume, had been amongst the first to find the empty tomb on Easter morning, were put on to an open boat 'without sail or oar', and, guided by Providence, arrived at this spot on the coast of Provence.

(Incidentally you can even find traces of these legends in Paris itself; every visitor to that great city admires the beautiful church of the Madeleine, and travellers by rail are familiar with the Gare St Lazare.) But to return to Saintes Maries de la Mer. Inside the church, which is a large fortress-like construction of the twelfth century, there is a primitive wood-carving which shows the two Marys sailing in their boat still carrying their vases of perfume! There are also relics of the saints preserved in the church which are the centre of great ceremonies three times a year.

Rather unexpectedly, however, even greater attention at Saintes Maries de la Mer is paid to another saint, St Sarah who, in another version of the legend, accompanied the two Marys as their servant, and in the course of the centuries has become the patron saint of gypsies. We never managed to discover how this had come about, but there can certainly be no doubt about it. During a period of 10 days in May each year, gypsies arrive in their thousands from all over the world. They come in every known form of transport, from traditional gypsy wagons to gleaming Cadillacs and Rolls-Royces. They take over the streets, squares and the seafront for a procession in honour of their patron saint. Her statue, clothed in multi-coloured robes and jewels, is venerated in the crypt of the church and then carried in triumph to the sea.

Apart from the very great interest of its historic church, however, the town of Saintes Maries de la Mer is a considerable disappointment. It has become totally engulfed in a vast development scheme which the French have designed to become a second Riviera and a rival for the tourist trade to the Spanish Costas.

However, there is a great deal more of major interest in the Camargue. The flat and marshy scenery makes a dramatic contrast to the rest of Provence. A large area is now a 'Parc Natural

Régional', and much of the former watery wilderness has been brought into cultivation for rice production, for which it was obviously suitable, but also more surprisingly for vines.

There are still lots of the picturesque pink flamingoes to be sighted, and white horses in plenty. The horses presumably are no longer genuinely wild, since there appears to be a flourishing tourist attraction in 'promenades à cheval', and the famous fighting bulls, we gathered, are now fewer in number and carefully controlled. Nevertheless, if you feel so inclined, you can even have a 'Visit to the Bulls on Horseback'. We were not tempted.

However, we did spend a most interesting morning at the Centre Ornithologique near Saintes Maries de la Mer. On display was a large collection of various kinds of hawks, buzzards, owls, herons and, of course, flamingoes. We were particularly delighted to find a huge storks' nest containing the parent birds and three young. An accompanying pamphlet explained that the parents in captivity had lost their migratory instinct, but the three young that they produced each year had not, and were allowed to fly away in the autumn.

This particularly interested us, since it confirmed something that we had learned in Alsace. There the huge storks' nests on church towers and other suitable sites have always been a prominent feature of the landscape. In recent years, however, the Alsatians, who are devoted to their storks, and regard them as harbingers of good luck, have been progressively more and more dismayed at their rapidly dwindling numbers.

Research had demonstrated that the birds were being killed for food, not surprisingly perhaps, as they flew over various hungry parts of Africa. So a vast experiment had been mounted in the village of Hunawihr. Dozens of the great birds were being detained in a huge cage in the open air, with facilities to nest and fly around freely, but not to migrate at the onset of winter. It had been established that after two years of this regime the birds lose their migratory instinct and their desire to fly to warmer climes. They are then released and generally return to their rooftop nests in various parts of Alsace.

We had intended to base ourselves in Saintes Maries de la Mer, but were put off by the unexpected commercialisation. Even the venerable church was surrounded by lurid bars and cheap-jack souvenir shops. But we found, happily, a total contrast in Aigues Mortes, a beautifully preserved little medieval city encircled by great walls very similar to those of Avila in Spain, and mercifully completely insulated from the creeping menace of the tourist development.

Aigues Mortes was more or less created at a stroke by King (Saint) Louis in the middle of the thirteenth century to serve as a port of embarkation for his Crusades. His statue stands in the small central square close to the church, which, like that of Saintes Maries, again looks much more like a fortress. St Louis was killed in 1270 and the walls and ramparts were completed by his son, Philip the Bold. They have been kept in good repair ever since, and for a small charge (and half that if you have the good fortune to be over 60 years of age), you can walk round the city on top of the walls. We followed this later with a stroll at ground level outside the walls, and were amazed to realise that still (in 1985) there had been virtually no overspill of the city beyond its medieval limits.

Not surprisingly, with all the stagnant water around, mosquitoes are evidently a menace in the Camargue in high summer. We had no such problems in June when we were there. Our attention was drawn to the potential problem, however, by watching ladies out shopping in Aigues Mortes happily chatting to their neighbours through the mosquito nets at their windows. It reminded us of visiting Carmelite nuns in their convent.

It was while we were travelling along one of those splendid minor roads that I mentioned earlier, that we were introduced quite by accident to another major amenity for the touring motorist in France. We were making our way from Vaison la Romaine to Fontaine de Vaucluse, one of the most famous beauty spots in the whole of Provence where the poet Petrarch sang in immortal verse of his unrequited love for Laura. We happened to notice a sign saying 'Le Vieux Moulin – Auberge Rurale'. It was then only mid-morning and we don't normally begin to look for accommodation for the night until late afternoon. But something prompted us to make enquiries.

We were greeted by a beaming, buxom Madame, and soon sensed that we might have chanced upon something rather special. 'But yes, certainly,' she said, we could have a double room with 'cabinet de toilette' and breakfast in the morning for about £10. However, there was clearly something much more important on her mind. Would we, she enquired anxiously, be returning for *le repas* in the evening? It would be a true Provencale meal, eaten out of doors in the warmth of a Mediterranean evening. With mounting excitement at the mere thought of these delights, she mentioned that there would be a 'ratatouille Provencale', and, as a further treat, her very own 'tarte aux fraises'. She enunciated each syllable of these sacred words slowly and deliberately in case we illiterate English had not grasped their significance.

We readily agreed that we could not possibly resist ratatouille *and* strawberry tart with wine included for the very modest price that she named. So, with a flurry of voluble French, she hoped that we would enjoy the beauties of nature that Provence possessed in such abundance and return with a *bon appétit*. We continued on our way with a pleasant sense of anticipation of a rewarding evening ahead.

Before that, however, there was Fontaine de Vaucluse which certainly lived up to its high reputation. The beauty spot is at the head of a rocky 'cirque' or what the geographers call a 'vallis clausa'. We were familiar with these from the Juras, where most of the rivers of the region seem to have their source in a mere trickle from an apparently solid rock-face. The beauty of Fontaine de Vaucluse was enhanced, when we were there in June, by masses of lavender on both banks of the River Sorgue, presenting a wonderful sight and scent.

So back to our auberge rurale. Dinner was late, but, of course, you expect that in the south of France, and even more so in Spain. Madame eventually appeared, vivacious and exuberant as before, bearing great dishes of 'hors d'oeuvres'. There followed pork chops with the famous 'ratatouille'. The 'tarte aux fraises' was more elaborate than she had indicated, being garnished with peaches and cherries as well. And to wash it all down, unlimited supplies of the local 'vin rouge'. There were a dozen or more people round the trestle table, and we struggled until nearly midnight in our very basic French to converse with our neighbours. They were all very patient and anxious to be kind and helpful to 'les Anglais'.

Encouraged by this splendid first experience, we kept our eyes open for similar places and soon realised that these 'chambres d'hôtes' were a serious rival to the excellent small hotels that I recommended earlier. The nearest English equivalent, perhaps, would be the generous hospitality that can be found in farmhouse accommodation in the Lake District. The French 'chambres d'hôtes', however, are organised on a national basis by the well-known Gites de France organisation, which monitors standards and fixes prices.

We were now ready for the last part of this tour of Provence. We had planned to follow in the steps of Napoléon, no less, along the celebrated Route Napoléon. 'They did it on foot. Let's do it by car!' says the brochure supplied by the Syndicat d'Initiative, the local Tourist Information Office. That was exactly what we had in mind.

It was on 1 March 1815, that the statesmen of Europe, assembled at the famous Congress of Vienna, were startled to learn that their arch-enemy, Napoléon, had escaped from prison on the island of Elba, and had landed on the French coast near Cannes. The place where he disembarked is marked with a commemorative stone on the front at Golfe Juan. With characteristic audacity, he made a bee-line for Paris, and with only a handful of men set off over rough mountain tracks through the Alps of Provence. Those mountain tracks are now a fine modern highway, Route Nationale N85, but you are never allowed to forget that this is still the historic Route Napoléon. Imperial eagles mark the way at every village; almost every hotel and restaurant includes 'Napoléon' or 'L'Empereur' in its name. Anyone returning from a holiday in the south of France or from Italy, and with a few days to spare, could be well advised to ignore the motorway and follow the Emperor's route through some stunning scenery packed with historical interest.

It is at Castellane, where Napoléon arrived at noon on 3 March that the scenery begins to be really dramatic. A chapel, perched on a sheer pinnacle of rock, inevitably reminds one of Le

Puy. Napoléon, of course, had little time for admiring the scenery, but anyone with business less pressing than reclaiming an empire, should note that Castellane is also the gateway to the Grand Canyon du Verdon, definitely one of the great scenic spectacles of Europe.

The name perhaps is unfortunate, inviting comparison inevitably with its American namesake. As far as France is concerned, however, having also toured the leading competitors, the Gorges of the Tarn, the Lot and the Ardèche, we can testify that for sheer scale and awesome grandeur, the Grand Canyon, in places nearly 2,300 feet deep, is in a class of its own. Baedeker, incredibly, suggests five hours for the round trip. Perhaps a mad French motorist who never stopped to look at the view, might manage that. Actually the Grand Canyon is well worth two circuits; one around the rim of the gorge, gazing down into the awesome depths, and a second one down in the gorge itself gazing up at the mighty crags. Both roads are perfectly manageable, and on the upper there are conveniently arranged pull-offs where one can safely stop to admire the scenery.

Realising that scenery of such magnificence deserved two or three days rather than Baedeker's five hours, we looked around for a convenient base from which to explore the Grand Canyon. With our usual good luck in France, we found it at the comfortable Auberge des Crêtes near La Palud. Here we had a double room with private shower and loo en suite and enormous meals at a remarkably reasonable price.

Back on the main road at Castellane, and slightly bemused after a surfeit of scenery and hairpin bends, we followed Napoléon again along a busy stretch of road through Digne to Sisteron, another picturesque little town dominated by an imposing medieval *citadelle*. The citizens of Sisteron take their historic moment of fame very seriously indeed, and produce a guide to the subject in the most extraordinary English.

This maintains that on Saturday, 4 March 1815, their forefathers held the fate of Europe in their hands. "Let the soldiers manning the guns on the citadel shoot at the man who madly attempts to rescue a crown, and no 100 days, no Waterloo, no craggy St Helena to await the moribund eagle.' The mayor and his entourage went out to confront the returning Emperor, but at the crucial moment the mayor's courage failed him, and he deemed it more prudent to welcome Napoléon rather than arrest him. Napoléon entered Sisteron unmolested, and remarked cheerfully to those around him, 'I am in Paris!'

If you fancy visiting the citadel, you can take a gaily-coloured little train from the town centre. You will still have several hundred steps to climb to the top. The view is tremendous, both to the south over the road along which Napoléon came to meet the mayor, and even better northwards to the mighty snow-covered Alps.

Then onwards through Gap and Corps and scenery that becomes steadily more impressive, to Laffrey. Here, at a point known as La Prairie de la Rencontre, Napoléon came face to face with the royalist troops sent to arrest him. He harangued them briefly and they quickly decided to join him rather than arrest him. This historic spot is marked with a fine equestrian statue. The Emperor now looks slightly green, and one doubts whether he would have approved of being fenced in with undignified railings. He would certainly have seen to it that the grass was kept in better order.

We stayed another night at the convenient Relais de l'Empereur. Next day we found ourselves negotiating La Descent de Laffrey, an incredibly steep gradient for a main road, with urgent warnings to keep in low gear for almost three miles into Vizille. The Emperor, of course, was on horseback, but how must his followers on foot have relished that headlong downhill dash after those forced marches through Alpine passes.

From Laffrey onwards it was one long triumphant progress for Napoléon through Grenoble and on to Paris. We could have picked up the motorway and got to Paris even more quickly than he did, but after all the excitement of the past week or so, we decided to stick to our favourite minor roads and loiter gently through Burgundy and the Beaujolais vineyards, and stock up with suitably priced bottles for the winter and the Christmas to come.

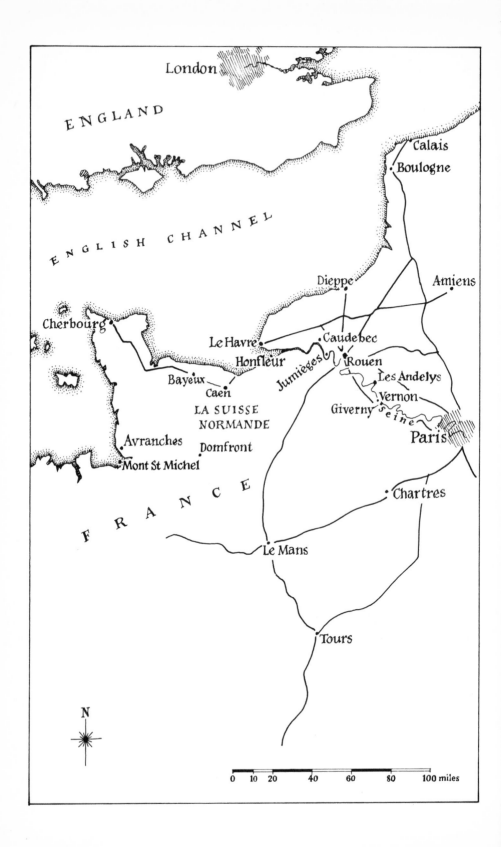

London

E N G L A N D

Calais
Boulogne

E N G L I S H C H A N N E L

Dieppe
Amiens

Cherbourg

Le Havre
Caudebec
Honfleur
Jumièges
Rouen
Les Andelys
Bayeux
Vernon
Caen
Giverny
Seine
LA SUISSE
NORMANDE
Paris

Avranches
Domfront
Mont St Michel

F R A N C E

Chartres

Le Mans

Tours

N

0 10 20   40   60   80   100 miles

CHAPTER TWO

France–Normandy

S
o often on our continental motoring holidays we have tended to regard Normandy and for that matter, the north of France in general, as somewhere to pass through quickly en route for more exciting places beyond, such as the Loire, the Dordogne or Provence. We have nevertheless been vaguely conscious of the fact that we were carelessly neglecting some areas of outstanding interest. Then one year we were returning to the coast from somewhere in the neighbourhood of Paris, and we happened to pick up a small publicity brochure entitled 'La Route Normandie Vexin' from one of those invaluable sources of information for travellers in France, a Syndicat d'Initiative, a Tourist Information Office.

All experienced wanderers around France are well aware that the French are remarkably dedicated to their official rural 'routes'. You may remember that we followed the most famous of these, the 'Route Napoléon', in the last chapter on Provence. However, there must be literally hundreds of them covering every region of the country. Each one is carefully planned and beautifully illustrated by local experts whose object, of course, is to convince the tourist of the unique beauties and historic attractions of their particular *département*.

The promoters of 'La Route Normandie Vexin' have an easy task of persuasion. The River Seine flows in spectacular loops from Paris north to Rouen, a matter of some 200 kilometres. Between these two famous cities no fewer than 15 sites are marked in the brochure as worthy of close attention along this 'route historique et culturelle'. We decided to postpone our return to the Channel port for an extra two or three days to have a leisurely look at just two of these places that particularly attracted us.

From Nantes through Vernon to Rouen the river flows majestically in great horseshoe bends beneath impressive overhanging cliffs. Here we located Les Andelys, which owes its plural name to the fact that it comprises two small towns about a kilometre apart, Le Petit Andely and Le Grand Andely. Le Petit is mainly notable for its extensive promenade along a particularly magnificent stretch of the river. Le Grand has a vast and splendid late thirteenth century church, 'one of the most important in France' according to a notice in the porch, and certainly as impressive as many a full-blown cathedral.

However, our main reason for visiting Les Andelys was to admire the massive Chateau Gaillard, categorised a 'monument historique et grand site national', a stark, gaunt, white ruin on a hilltop, which dominates the landscape for miles around. This huge castle was, unbelievably, constructed in a single year on the orders of Richard Coeur de Lion, King of England and Duke of Normandy, in order to bar the King of France from access to the sea.

Despite the fact that the afore-mentioned brochure indicates opening hours and 'visites guidées', when we were there in June, access appeared to be open and free of charge at any time. The young and energetic, therefore, can scramble up to the castle by any of several paths from both the Andelys. By car you follow a tortuous one-way road from the centre of Le Grand Andely, with many hairpin bends and the last 300 metres extremely steep. To be honest, I'm not absolutely sure that it's entirely worth the trouble, since the castle at close quarters is not as magnificent and awe-inspiring as when viewed from below, but the view in reverse over the great horseshoe bend of the river is indeed *magnifique*.

The brochure, as mentioned before, would have us visit 14 more 'Hauts-Lieux', all historical and cultural, including seven more chateaux and a brace of abbeys. We decided to concentrate instead on just one of the 14, the house and garden of the *maitre incontesté* of the Impressionist movement, the great artist, Claude Monet. The house is easily located at the little village of Giverny, close to the large town of Vernon.

After a turbulent earlier career, Monet settled in this house in 1883. Seven years later he acquired a strip of marshland across the road, and began to construct his renowned water-lily garden which became the subject of some of his most famous canvasses. His painter colleagues, indeed, considered his garden to be itself one of his most important works of art, the equal of his pictures that now command many millions of francs. The house and garden were later bequeathed by his son to the French nation, and now, restored to their original magnificence, rank as a 'Monument National'.

The garden simply exceeds all expectations. Never have we seen such a riot of colour. It connects via an underpass with the celebrated 'Etang des Lilas', the water-garden with superb weeping willows, wisteria, Japanese bridges and of course, the water-lilies. Amateur photographers by the dozen were jostling for position to get an exact reproduction of their favourite Monet original.

The house on the other hand is relatively disappointing. There are no Monet original paintings on display as one might have expected. Instead, several of the rooms have their walls hung with Japanese prints, of which the artist was apparently an enthusiastic collector. Finally, as with many National Trust properties in England, there is a shop near the entrance which, when we were there, was doing a roaring trade in Impressionist prints in all shapes and sizes and Monet memorabilia of every kind.

This visit to Giverny and Monet's marvellous garden turned out to be one of the most memorable and certainly most colourful days that we had enjoyed in all our wanderings around France. As we drove northwards again towards the Hovercraft at Boulogne, we made a firm resolve that our next trip to France would take the form of a tour in depth of other parts of Normandy. When we were later planning this expedition, we decided that we would largely ignore the popular seaside holiday resorts and the large cities such as Rouen and Caen, and concentrate rather on the less-known inland areas.

On arrival we soon discovered that a tourist in these northern parts of Normandy is going to find his travels dominated by memories of two historic invasions separated by almost a thousand years, and launched in opposite directions. The date 1066 is one that no English schoolboy fails to remember, and 1944 is the date that no Frenchman, and no Norman in particular, will ever forget.

It was in June 1944 that millions of men-at-arms and the

destructive power of modern war brought utter devastation to the normally peaceful fields and villages of Normandy. Memorials of those dreadful days are inevitably in evidence on all sides. Strangely enough, apart from the landing beaches themselves, now ironically major tourist attractions, present-day Normandy seems to place rather more emphasis on 'Guillaume le Conquérant' and his historic invasion in the opposite direction.

We first met up with William at the ruined abbey of Jumièges, situated in that remarkable horseshoe bend of the River Seine west of Rouen. We learned to our great surprise that William was definitely present at the consecration of the abbey in 1067. It rather looks as if '1066 and All That' caused him considerably less trouble and was far less time-consuming than our history books had led us to believe.

Jumièges was deliberately destroyed during the French Revolution and is now just a huge, romantic ruin, rather reminiscent of our own Fountains Abbey in the sheer extent of the ruins and the beauty of its situation. The modest entrance fee is suitably reduced for pensioners or members of what the French gracefully call *La Troisième Age*.

Only 12 kilometres further down the stream is another great abbey, that of St Wandrille, part ruin, but mainly restored, and since 1969 in full occupation again by Benedictine monks whose Order founded it in 649. The present buildings date mainly from the eleventh and twelfth centuries, with the curious addition of a huge fifteenth century wooden barn transplanted from a nearby village and transformed into an impressive monastery church.

Almost as interesting and impressive as these two great abbeys is the Eglise St Marie of nearby Caudebec, with flamboyant flying buttresses and situated just alongside the colourful and majestic modern bridge over the Seine, the Pont de Brotonne. Eglise St Marie is no ordinary parish church. As we entered, we were greeted by a quotation from King Henri IV of France who described it as 'the most beautiful chapel of my kingdom'. A further notice informs visitors that 'more than 300 little personages, angels, musicians, prophets, saints, clergy, bourgeoisie and men in the street have welcomed you, sculpted over the main entrance'. In the same manner the whole great church is most commendably cared for and documented. Details of the magnificent medieval stained glass in 18 separate chapels are all described and elucidated *in situ*. There is a final word of praise for the organ which, 'with remarkable sonority has since 1547 accompanied the faithful in their chants and their prayers'.

We visited the church and the two abbeys from one of the most remarkably cheap hotels we have ever come across even in France. 'Le Grand Sapin' in Villequier near Caudebec, a lovely rambling, even slightly ramshackle old place, with a wooden balcony overlooking the Seine, provided us with a double room with private loo plus an excellent meal for surprisingly few francs.

Nor should the church in Villequier be overlooked, if only for the graves in the churchyard of the family of Victor Hugo. This placid stretch of the River Seine was the scene of a terrible tragedy, when the great writer's 19-year-old daughter and her husband were both drowned in a boating accident only six months after their marriage. Nearby there is a statue of Victor Hugo gazing mournfully over the fatal spot.

It is at Falaise and Bayeux that the Conqueror really comes into his own. Falaise suffered terribly in the last war, but for a small charge you can still visit the remains of the chateau where he was born, and where he later planned the invasion of England. Near the entrance there stands the famous equestrian statue of him which appears in most of the guide books and brochures; it was erected by national (Norman) subscription in 1851, and somehow survived 1944.

The celebrated Bayeux Tapestry, which is actually not tapestry but embroidery is, of course, a unique historical record and deserves every five-star treatment. At the 'Musée Guillaume le Conquérant' in Bayeux it certainly gets it. If you are planning a visit allow a full half-day, since even in May there were great crowds queuing for admission. The museum is open every day from 9 am till 7 pm. There are regrettably no concessions for pensioners.

The visit is in three stages. You are first of all introduced to an exhibition in which the historical background of Saxons, Danes and Normans is exhaustively explained by reference to various contemporary sources. Next you move on to a 15-minute cinema show, alternately in French and English, in which the educational process is continued audio-visually. Finally you come to the 'Tapisserie de la Reine Mathilde' itself, inevitably encased, but surprisingly well-lit. It is thought that the work was embroidered in coloured wools for the consecration of Bayeux Cathedral in 1077. The brilliance of the coloured wools has scarcely faded over the centuries. The emphasis in the story that the tapestry tells is again rather different from what you and I learned in the history books. The pictures, which are surprisingly clear and frequently amusing, are accompanied by a Latin commentary, and together they tell this story:

Edward the Confessor bequeaths his kingdom to his cousin, William Duke of Normandy. Harold, his Commander-in-Chief, swears an oath to accept William as the next King of England. Harold nevertheless seizes the throne for himself. Thereupon William, grievously wronged, crosses the Channel to claim his righteous inheritance. The treacherous and perjured Harold then gets his well-deserved come-uppance.

Even if there were no tapestry, Bayeux would still be well worth a leisurely visit for an inspection of its magnificent cathedral alone. Internally it is exceptionally light, and, as with the church at Caudebec, all the main features of interest are carefully brought to the attention of visitors and helpfully explained. Bayeux, a mere 12 kilometres from the invasion beaches of 'D Day', miraculously survived the war unscathed, with its priceless memento of the earlier invasion in the opposite direction preserved for posterity. Proud memories of Guillaume le Conquérant would still seem to reign supreme in Normandy.

There was another area of inland Normandy that we were anxious to explore, largely because we were intrigued by its curious name, 'La Suisse Normande'. It lies along the valley of the River Orne, a few kilometres south of the city of Caen, and owes its strange name to the deep gorges and rocky escarpments that give a picturesque and mildly mountainous appearance, quite different from the flat, pastoral plains of most of Normandy.

The guide books tend to scoff at its pretentious title, since there is certainly nowhere in Normandy anything remotely comparable to the snowy peaks and passes of Alpine Switzerland. We didn't think the name quite so inappropriate, however; the area reminded us very strongly of that part of Switzerland where the Jura mountains straddle the border with France. The winding Orne, with its pretty waterfalls and masses of wild flowers adorning its banks, was to us very reminiscent of the Doubs or the Loue, or the many other rivers that flow through similar scenery in the Juras.

The best of the scenery can be enjoyed by following yet another French rural 'route'. The well-signposted 'Route de la Suisse Normande' escorts you round a series of very minor roads through extremely beautiful country from Thury Harcourt in the north, via Clecy and Pont d'Ouilly to Putanges in the south. On the way you can admire a remarkable range of hazardous-looking outdoor pursuits for which the valley has become very popular. Rock-climbing, canoeing, water-skiing and hang-gliding were all happening as we drove along the valley.

On the Sunday we attended Mass in the village church at Putanges. Quite a large congregation was assembling as we entered, and a sort of Master of Ceremonies was busily organising the choir, organist and lay readers. Observing that there were visitors present, he came across to us and courteously invited me to read one of the lessons. 'Ah, mais non, monsieur,' I modestly replied, 'je suis anglais, et je ne parle pas francais très bien'. He remained unconvinced, and pressed the invitation, but I thought it prudent to ask to be excused.

The memorable day that we had spent at Giverny admiring Monet's marvellous garden had stimulated still further our interest, already considerable, in Impressionist painting. As a result we decided that there was one other place in Normandy that we couldn't afford to miss while we had the opportunity, namely the picturesque port of Honfleur.

With a long and eventful history, Honfleur is now a major tourist attraction. Few such resorts, however, can have enjoyed so much free publicity of such very high quality. Four of the greatest of the French Impressionists, Monet, Renoir, Pissarro and Cezanne, lived and worked there at one time or another, and featured scenes of Honfleur in their pictures. A fifth, Boudin, Monet's teacher, was born in Honfleur and worked there all his life.

There is now a magnificent 'Musée Eugène Boudin', purpose-built and presented to the town by a wealthy, art-loving citizen. The gallery is beautifully furnished and decorated with masses of plants and flowers, and makes a most worthy setting for the many works of Boudin and other Impressionist and post-Impressionist painters that it proudly displays. There was a specially reduced entrance fee for students and the over-60s. The latter were supposed to provide proof of eligibility for the reduction. We had no such proof with us, but one glance satisfied the kind lady in the ticket office that we qualified!

Old harbours, even those deserted except for small fishing boats and pleasure craft, seem always so remarkably attractive and photogenic. The old part of the harbour of Honfleur is almost absurdly picturesque, with colourful houses six or seven storeys high flanking 'le vieux bassin,' once the flourishing heart of a busy commercial port. It is also steeped in history, not only French, but equally English, Canadian and American.

For instance, on the wall of the ancient 'Lieutenance', the gateway to the inner harbour, there is a tablet to the memory of Samuel de Champlain. It records that with boats and equipment from the port of Honfleur, he explored Canada and Acadia from 1603 to 1607. Then, sailing from the same port in 1608, he founded the city of Quebec. Very near the 'Lieutenance' is the town's most remarkable building, the Church of St Catherine, which has a detached belfry. Both were intended to be only temporary buildings but, despite being constructed almost entirely of wood, have defied the potential ravages of fire, dry rot and woodworm, and survived for over 500 years.

Because of its strategic but exposed situation at the mouth of the Seine, Honfleur was regularly the target of pirates and marauders of many races and especially, of course, the English. Apparently our impious ancestors completely destroyed the previous St Catherine's during the Hundred Years' War. Since the citizens of Honfleur had no money with which to rebuild their church in the conventional way, they turned to the skills of their naval craftsmen and the plentiful timber in the neighbouring forests to build a replacement in wood.

Most unusually, they designed the new church with two parallel naves and, using their shipbuilding techniques, a roof that looks exactly like the upturned hull of a boat. The church also houses an historic organ of 1771 with sculptured panels depicting musical instruments of the period such as serpent, bugle-horn and hurdy-gurdy. The separate belfry, one of Monet's favourite subjects, is now a museum of religious art.

The artistic heritage of Honfleur clearly lingers on. There are numerous minor galleries and exhibitions, and shops selling pictures, paints, canvasses and miscellaneous artists' requirements. Everywhere around the quays we came upon artists at their easels still reproducing those same scenes that inspired Boudin, Monet and the rest of the Impressionists over a hundred years ago.

We made our day trip to Honfleur while staying at an excellent 'chambre d'hôte', a farmhouse at Le Sap, near Vimoutier. That memorable evening that we had so much enjoyed at the 'auberge rurale' near Fontaine de Vaucluse, that I described in the previous chapter on Provence, had led us to investigate more fully the possibilities of this form of accommodation. We discovered that there were literally thousands of them scattered all over the country, but centrally supervised by the well-known 'Gites de France' organisation which controls the prices and monitors the standards. The full 'Chambres d'Hôtes Book' can be obtained from the French National Tourist Office in Piccadilly, London. Departmental lists can be picked up at local 'Syndicat d'Initiative' offices as you go along.

As we emerged from our car on our first arrival at Le Sap, we were greeted by our beaming hostess. 'Enchantée', she said, and escorted us to a large airy room with all possible mod cons provided. In the evening we dined *en famille* with the farmer and his wife. Monsieur Bourgault cordially invited us to join him in an apéritif. On the table there were plentiful bottles of 'vin rouge' which we came to realise later was standard fare in 'chambres d'hôtes', but at Le Sap there was home-brewed Normandy cider as well.

When we complimented Monsieur on his wife's cuisine, which was superb, he remarked solemnly 'Mais oui, monsieur, c'est vrai; en France c'est bien boire et bien manger'. (In France we eat well and drink well!) Then, to prove the point, he insisted that we join him in a concluding liqueur — all on the house! — and as we were leaving next morning we were presented with several bottles of the home brew to take home with us!

Perhaps I might be allowed at this point to digress a little to describe a few more of the interesting experiences we enjoyed in 'chambres d'hôtes' in various parts of France. There was for, instance, the farmhouse accommodation deep in the country in the region of Riberac in the Dordogne. On a pre-prandial stroll we noticed a large gaggle of geese and goslings, which was obviously one of the main enterprises of the farm.

Later we found that we were the only guests, and dined alone with the farmer and his wife. The first course was an interesting vegetable soup. To our astonishment and amusement, the farmer, who was a very friendly, genial old boy, having finished his soup, proceeded to refill his soup bowl with 'vin rouge' from the bottle on the table. He cordially invited us to do the same. Noticing that his wife smiled indulgently at him but did not follow his example, we politely declined. He was clearly disappointed, and explained that this curious procedure was a custom of the region.

We were in the middle of the next pleasant course, a delicious casserole of goose, when the wife suddenly leaped up from her chair screaming 'Le reynard, le reynard!' and dashed outside. She had spotted a fox through the window, and hastened to check that the precious geese and their goslings were all safely protected from the marauder. Never a dull moment at a 'chambre d'hôte'!

On another occasion, at a sort of mini-chateau in central France ('chambres d'hôtes' come in many different guises), we found ourselves sharing a table with a venerable and serious-minded veteran from Alsace who was also on a touring holiday with his wife. The old gentleman was clearly anxious to take the opportunity to get the views of 'les anglais' on a number of topics. He began by inviting our opinions on 'le tunnel', which he suggested would greatly improve international relations and reduce the notorious insularity of the British. We indicated that we thought the Channel Tunnel on the whole to be a good thing.

Having broken the ice, he then posed the question that was

Having broken the ice, he then posed the question that was clearly uppermost in his mind. What, he enquired, did we think of 'La dame de fer'? When we cautiously indicated that we were not amongst Mrs Thatcher's greatest admirers he was obviously pleased, and solemnly declared 'Avec la dame de fer, les riches seront plus riches, et les pauvres seront plus pauvres' (with the Iron Lady, the rich will get richer, and the poor poorer.) Again we could only agree.

We thought it reasonable to ask him in return for his opinion of President Mitterand. He replied with alacrity. 'When he was first a candidate for the presidency, I thought I cannot vote for Giscard, like La dame de fer, he is too arrogant. But I cannot vote for Mitterand, he will ruin the economy. So what did I do? I went fishing!'

The 'chambre d'hôte' at Le Sap is at some distance from the small village of that name, and is found at the end of a very minor road really not much more than a cart-track. The nearest small town is Vimoutier, a pleasant little place where we found in the village square an unexpected memorial, a statue not to the usual local worthy, but to Marie Harel, the inventor, if that is the right word, of that gourmet delicacy, Camembert cheese! An inscription informed us that the statue had been paid for by grateful cheese manufacturers from Ohio, USA.

Marie Harel, we discovered, lived at the neighbouring village of Camembert, so we thought we should go and have a look at it. We found this minuscule village *en fete* with streamers and bunting all around. There is even another route, 'la route du Camembert'. We couldn't imagine what there was to see except perhaps a chance to admire the cows that have the privilege of contributing their milk to the famous cheese. We thought that we should at least buy some of the authentic product to present to friends back at home. Our luggage, however, seemed somewhat odoriferous before we reached home some weeks later.

Despite our firm resolve to avoid the well-known cities and tourist centres in our exploration of Normandy, we felt that we simply had to make one exception, the famous and utterly unique, Mont St Michel. In fact, with the exception of Paris and Versailles, Mont St Michel on the borders of Normandy and Brittany, receives more tourists every year than any other place in France. Understandably so, since the Mount is without question one of the great sights of Europe.

The first glimpse from a distance of that tapering pyramid of granite, apparently rising straight out of the sea, is a thrill that few other sights can equal. On closer inspection one's rapture is slightly modified. In no real sense is the Mount any longer an island, since it is joined to the mainland by a causeway that is submerged only at the highest equinoctial tides. The approach by car is rather reminiscent of the road to Venice. At the end of the causeway one has no alternative than to use the official car park. It is comforting, however, to read this prominent notice 'Today the sea will not cover this parking'. One then enters the Mount through an ancient fortification, the Barbican, and ascends the 'Grande Rue' which is the only road to the church known appropriately as 'La Merveille', and the monastery above.

It was all of 25 years since our only previous visit to Mont St Michel, and this time the gradient seemed strangely much steeper than we had remembered, and we had certainly forgotten that there are 365 steps to the entrance to the abbey. Indeed, one writer has calculated that a complete tour of all the extensive buildings involves tackling more like 900 steps!

However, at least this exhausting ascent provides a good excuse for frequent pauses to gaze in wonder at the incredible feat of medieval engineering that contrived to place this massive monument on such a tiny pinnacle of rock — a feat all the more remarkable since the Mount at that time was still genuinely an island. Having at last struggled up to the abbey church you pay quite a stiff entrance fee, reduced, however, for the over-60s. (We ruefully reflected that the authorities no doubt count on the latter being comparatively few in number.) Only guided tours are permitted.

We have suffered a lot over the years from a remarkable assortment of bad guides. The worst are certainly the Germans, many of whom we have suspected to be descendants of W.S. Gilbert's 'mystical Germans who preach from ten to four'. Quite the most amusing was a little Italian at the Palace of Caserta — but that must really wait till Part Two of this book. Back at Mont St Michel our guide was a sweet young girl with hopelessly inadequate English, who seemed to be perpetually groping for the *mot juste* to complete her sentence. We got very impatient with her shortcomings, but finally felt rather ashamed of ourselves when, at the end of the tour, she naively apologised and explained that it had been her very first attempt at the job!

However, little assistance is needed to appreciate the architectural wonders of this amazing building, so aptly named 'The Marvel', and which seems almost incredibly poised in space. One can well understand why the French writer Maupassant described it as 'That gigantic granite jewel as delicate as a piece of lacework, the most wonderful Gothic building ever made for God on earth'.

As with most places of pilgrimage, one simply has to ignore the rampant commercialism, as one pushes past endless souvenir shops, fast food dives and the like. But our breath really was taken away by the sheer effrontery of the prices of the famous hotel 'La Mère Poulard'. Mother Poulard is credited with having invented the fluffy omelette that is so popular all over Normandy and Brittany. For the privilege of dining at this historic spot one paid £35 (1988 prices) for the standard menu. If you were prepared for a little self-denial, you could have the 'Pilgrim Menu' for £27. A rock bottom possibility, called curiously 'A menu around an omelette', cost a mere £14.50. A room for the night ranged from £35 to £85. I leave the reader to calculate what these prices will be since 'Black Wednesday'. If you are prepared to haul yourself and your belongings to the top of the 'Grande Rue', there are more hotels at more normal rates. Incidentally, Mother Poulard's prices seemed all the more outrageous when we observed that along the road to the Mount from nearby Pontorson we passed a positive rash of perfectly acceptable places offering meals from £5 to £6 and rooms at around £10.

To see Mont St Michel to the very best advantage, one should time one's arrival to coincide with the equinoctial high tides in March and September, when great waves sweep round the bay in spectacular manner and the Mount again becomes an island. The abbey has inevitably suffered many vicissitudes over the centuries. In 1790 it was finally dissolved and experienced the humiliation under Napoléon of becoming a prison. Better times have returned, however. Since 1969 six Bendictine monks have been in residence, and Mass is celebrated each day at 12.15 pm.

Visitors to Mont St Michel can find much else in the vicinity to interest them. For instance, Avranches, a mere 10 miles away to the east, is a fascinating place for any student of history, ancient, medieval or modern. Its museum contains a priceless collection of manuscripts, including the earliest known text of the Roman orator Cicero, another of Abelard, and a tenth century history of the Abbey of St Michel. From the Jardin de Plantes in Avranches there is also a magnificent view of the Mount across the bay.

Travellers around Europe who rightly marvel at the size and complexity of medieval cathedrals can easily overlook the fact that not all their architects were uniformly expert. Avranches is apparently a case in point; its eleventh century cathedral simply collapsed when under attack during the French Revolution. All that now remains is a historic stump of a pillar fenced off with chains, and known as the 'plate forme'. An inscription reads:

> 'On this stone at the door of the Cathedral of Avranches, after the murder of St Thomas à Becket, Archbishop of Canterbury, Henry II, King of England and Duke of Normandy, received on his knees from the legate of the Pope the apostolic absolution on Sunday the 21st of March, 1172.'

Not far away is a memorial to other historic events more than seven centuries later. On soil which was solemnly designated American in perpetuity, there stands a monument to General 'Blood and Guts' Patton, on the spot where he planned the breakthrough from the landing beaches which was to carry his troops to Paris and beyond in 1944.

Anyone whose interest in Thomas à Becket has been stimulated by the 'plate forme' in Avranches should certainly make the short journey to Domfront, a pleasant little town which is almost entirely ignored by the guide books. Nevertheless it has a ruined château of immense historical significance. A helpful notice at the entrance explains that it was built by Henry I and was the birthplace of

Eleanor of Aquitaine, wife of Henry II, mother of Richard Coeur de Lion and grandmother of St Louis of France. Eleanor is often ranked by historians as the most powerful woman of the Middle Ages. Cinema-goers will remember her portrayed by Kathryn Hepburn in *The Lion in Winter*. The notice goes on to tell us that the castle survived some 20 sieges over the centuries, and was finally demolished in 1608 on the orders of Sully, minister of Henry IV.

But to return to Thomas à Becket. He was a guest here during his brief exile in France, and actually said Mass on Christmas Day at the Church of Notre Dame sur l'Eau alongside the River Cance at the bottom of the hill from the chateau. The altar at which he presided is a treasured relic and still in use in the church to this day.

Having warned you off the hotels of Mont St Michel, I will now reveal our ideal solution, another magnificent 'chambre d'hôte' only 12 miles from the Mount at Vergoncey near St James. 'La Ferme de l'Etang' is a farmhouse overlooking a beautiful small lake. Madame Gavard provided us with a large double room and superb five-course table d'hôte dinners with cider, wine and liqueurs included, for a fraction of the charge of the outrageous Madame Poulard on the Mount. On our initial visit we had intended staying one night, but made it four. We have found excuses for returning in later years, and so have other members of our family.

N

Venice

Bologna

ADRIATIC
SEA

Lucca
Pisa
Pistoia
Florence
Livorno
TUSCANY
Arezzo
Volterra
San
Gimignano
Gubbio
Siena
Cortona
Lake
Trasimeno
Perugia
Assisi
UMBRIA
Todi
Orvieto
Spoleto

TYRRHENIAN
SEA

Rome

0 10 20   40   60   80   100 miles

CHAPTER THREE

Italy–Tuscany and Umbria

T here can be no possible doubt that the top priorities in Italy
for any intelligent tourist must be the big cities. On the
other hand, Rome, Milan, Florence and Venice are no
places for motorists, except the most intrepid and
masochistic. In any case the Roman Forum, the Colosseum, St
Peter's, the Vatican, like the art galleries and Renaissance monuments of Florence, can only be appreciated adequately on foot, sup-
plemented where desirable by the occasional bus or taxi. As for
Venice, a motorist has no option but to abandon his car in a huge car
park outside the city and proceed by boat. So for the big cities other
means of access — train, plane and package tour — are clearly the
answer. When the incomparable riches of these big cities have been
at last exhausted, however, there remains still a great wealth of historic, artistic and scenic interest to be discovered by the itinerant
motorist in the smaller, quieter towns and villages of Italy.

Nowhere is this truer than amongst the hill towns of Tuscany
and Umbria, set amidst the glorious scenery of the Appennines. We
decided to make the area one of our first retirement expeditions,
but first of all, of course, we had to get there. Our car at the time
was actually a Mini, to which we were affectionately and perhaps
unreasonably devoted. We were not particularly intimidated by the
prospect of taking the Mini across the Alps, because we had made a
couple of similar trips in pre-retirement days. We had exchanged
our house for the summer holidays two years running with an Italian
architect who lent us a delightful holiday bungalow, naturally
architect designed, in the foothills of the Dolomites.

On the first occasion we found no particular problems negotiating the St Gothard Pass. In fact, I remember sending a postcard back
home claiming that the pass was no more formidable than the local
Trough of Bowland. (For the benefit of possibly ill-informed

southerners who imagine that Lancashire is all 'dark Satanic mills', I should explain that the Trough of Bowland is a highly scenic pass connecting the beauties of the Ribble Valley with Lancaster and the even finer scenery of the Lake District.)

The next year we used the less well-known Arlberg Pass, which proved equally manageable. Of course, motorists who don't fancy mountains at all can make use instead of one of the many tunnels that now run under the Alps. We've used the Mont Blanc tunnel once or twice and found it no more difficult than the Mersey Tunnel though, of course, several times as long. Finally one could use in reverse the grand 'Route Napoléon' described in the first chapter, and continue on the motorway round the coast from the Riviera. Whatever our ultimate destination, we always try to make a virtue out of a necessity, and enjoy the journey as part of the holiday. This year we had decided to use the Simplon Pass, which starts from the upper valley of the Rhône in Switzerland, and to linger en route in a few favourite places in the lovely French Juras. Then via Geneva into Switzerland towards the Simplon.

It was in the neighbourhood of Martigny in Switzerland that the Mini began to develop a disturbing tendency to stall. With a hard day's journey in prospect on the next day, I decided that we'd better have something done about it. We drew into a garage and I explained to the proprietor the problem as best I could, and my concern in view of the Alps and Italy ahead on the morrow. He immediately summoned a mechanic and together they tinkered around under the bonnet for a quarter of an hour or so, and then triumphantly emerged to pronounce that all was well. They were obviously delighted to oblige, wished us 'bonnes vacances', and firmly refused to accept a penny or even a franc for their trouble.

We spent the night at a small Swiss hotel in the mountain village of Leuk. For dinner, Madame urged us to try fondue, 'la specialité Suisse'. So we had a rather expensive and not very satisfying meal in which we monotonously speared pieces of different kinds of bread and dipped them into hot liquid cheese. More cheese with Germanic black bread for breakfast next morning, after which we set off at last for the Simplon Pass. This proved to be surprisingly straightforward, with relatively few hairpin bends, and gradients which permitted top gear for much of the way. After the Swiss mechanic's ministrations, the Mini positively scampered to the top at over 6,000 feet.

Thereafter a gentle drive downhill into Italy with a pause for a picnic by the shore of Lake Orta. Next a rather dismal industrialised area, till around Alessandria the autostrada materialised, after which it was a long spectacular drive with alternating viaducts and 'gallerie' along the Mediterranean coast around Genoa, till we finally stopped at Rapallo for the night.

Next morning back on to the autostrada, with more of the viaducts and 'gallerie' along the coast and later through lush countryside, until we left it past Pontedera for our first Tuscan hill town, Volterra, which proved an excellent start to our tour. Volterra, on its superb site, is a centre of Etruscan antiquities. The Etruscans, according to Herodotus (who is never to be trusted very much), came from Lydia in Asia Minor. They certainly established their own distinctive civilisation in this part of Italy about the same time that the Greeks were colonising 'magna Graecia'. Later, of course, they were both absorbed by the Romans.

The Etruscan town walls still survive in Volterra and the museum is full of Etruscan antiquities, particularly alabaster cremation urns. However, the fine buildings in the town centre are mainly from a much later medieval period, and to this day the alabaster industry remains the town's main source of employment.

Only a few miles from Volterra is the remarkable city of San Gimignano. We have come across quite a number of places in our travels claiming to be the 'best preserved medieval city in Europe' — Chinon in the Loire Valley, Sos del Re Catolico in the Spanish Pyrenees, and several along the 'Romantische Strasse' in Germany, to name just a few. But San Gimignano must definitely be high on the short-list in this particular beauty competition.

As you approach San Gimignano from a distance you are astonished to see a veritable forest of towers of various sizes. There are actually 12 of them (Baedeker) or 13 (Michelin and Fodor). It all depends on whether you count one particularly sawn-off specimen. The original number has been variously estimated as between 56 (Baedeker) 72 (Michelin) and 79 (Fodor!).

The spectacle is certainly bizarre in the extreme. The towers are the remains, apparently, of a sort of medieval 'keeping up with the Joneses', when each important citizen felt it essential to his prestige to build a tower to his property higher than any of his neighbours. These incredible towers in their setting of lovely medieval streets and squares, plus a fine Romanesque cathedral with notable frescoes by several fourteenth century masters, makes San Gimignano stand out in our memory as one of the most picturesque places we have ever visited.

We felt that we could not resist including a visit to Siena, since we were so near, although it does not strictly come into the category of small hill towns, since it straddles three small hills and is almost a major city. However, it boasts two magnificent show-pieces which no tourist in Tuscany would want to miss. The first is its superb cathedral, surely one of the most spectacular in Europe, with its marble exterior in red, white and black stripes, its unique floor of inlaid marble, and its celebrated Piccolomini Chapel with sixteenth century frescoes by Pinturicchio.

Siena's other show-piece is its vast Piazza del Campo, one of the finest squares in Italy, rivalled in size only by St Peter's in Rome and St Mark's in Venice. Here there takes place twice in the summer the sensational 'Corso del Palio', a weird horse race round the Campo, with participants in medieval costume, and absolutely no holds barred, which rouses huge crowds of spectators to frenzies of excitement.

Cortona, perched on another great hill is now one of the smallest of the hill towns of Tuscany. From its ancient ramparts it commands tremendous views over the Appennines. In its churches and museums it is still the proud custodian of some glorious works of art, including masterpieces of Fra Angelico and many paintings by Signorelli, who was a native of Cortona. The appearance of Cortona's streets and squares can have changed very little since the days of the Renaissance.

It was on our way from Cortona to Perugia that we found an unusually memorable site for our midday picnic by the shore of Lake Trasimeme. It was all very peaceful with a heat haze partially obscuring the view. We recalled that it was on such a day in June

217 BC that the famous Carthaginian general Hannibal inflicted at this place one of the worst defeats ever suffered by a Roman army. It was quite awe-inspiring to imagine the legions of Gaius Flaminius marching all unsuspecting through the narrow pass between the mountains and the lake, and the Carthaginians descending on them from the hills above with such terrible effect that, according to Livy, the lake turned red with Roman blood.

Hannibal followed this with an even more crushing victory the following year at Cannae, and Rome, totally exhausted, lay at his mercy. Hannibal strangely did not seem to realise this, and never attacked the city itself. 'Vincere scis, Hannibal, victoria uti nescis' ('You know how to win victories, Hannibal, but you don't know how to use them'), said his second-in-command, Maharbal, according to the historian Livy. This fascinating picnic site took me back some 50 years to when my university professor of ancient history was wont to speculate on the subsequent course of history if Hannibal *had* marched on Rome. We might have had a quite different way of life today, and even be speaking a different language!

And so on into Umbria. Perugia and Assisi are undoubtedly the top tourist attractions of Umbria but were not on the itinerary of this tour by car, mainly because we had explored them in some depth a few years previously on a tour by train. As we by-passed Perugia on our way to Todi and Orvieto through still more superb scenery, we could not help recalling a most remarkable and entertaining musical experience that happened to us in Perugia.

On that occasion we were wandering around that extremely interesting city when we noticed large posters advertising a one-off performance at the Opera House in Perugia of the two one-act operas, *Cavalleria Rusticana* by Mascagni and *I Pagliacci* by Leoncavallo, known affectionately to generations of opera goers as Cav and Pag. In enormous letters we were informed that there would be a guest appearance by the celebrated 'tenore robusto', Mario del Monaco.

We had heard del Monaco on records, and knew that he was possibly the Italians' favourite tenor in the period between Gigli and Pavarotti. He was particularly noted for the sheer size of his voice; it was of him that a wit once remarked that he was not so much an exponent of 'bel canto' as of 'can belto'! On application to the box office we were pleased to find that there were still seats available, but only in the 'ultimo piano', which we took to mean the 'gods'.

Indeed on the night we ascended seemingly endless flights of stairs, but finally emerged, not into the expected English type gods, but into a small box seemingly glued to the ceiling of the Opera House. From this vantage point we had an excellent view not merely of the stage, but also of the rest of the audience, and the audience in Italy can be as entertaining as the performers. Cav came first, but without Mario del Monaco; he was approaching the end of his career and was obviously saving himself for his big moment in Pag. It was a most curious production. The orchestra and soloists were top-class professionals from Florence. However the chorus was from the local amateur choral society, was dressed the same for both operas, and made no pretence whatsoever of acting, but simply stood still in rows like the chorus in *Messiah* back home.

When del Monaco finally made his appearance in Pag, the action was held up for a couple of minutes while he was accorded a hero's welcome. When he later sang the great aria 'Vesti la giubba' and the last Caruso-type sob had died away, absolutely all hell was let loose and the whole theatre positively erupted. The orchestra meanwhile pressed on stoically with the fairly lengthy and lovely coda that follows; they could not have heard a single note of what they were playing. At the end of the performance the great man received a prolonged standing ovation that would have put to shame even a Tory Party conference.

If I may extend a little further this musical digression, music lovers desirous of hearing Italian opera at its best, and quite rightly deterred by the ruinous prices of La Scala Milan and the opera houses of the other big cities, should contrive to be holidaying within reach of Verona during the months of July and August. We were in the neighbourhood with the family in the two years before retirement, and hastened to get tickets for the world-famous open-air opera in the ancient Roman arena. Built in AD 100, and beginning presumably with gladiators, if not Christians and lions, it has housed entertainment of some kind ever since.

If one uses the simile of an old-fashioned football stadium, this enormous arena can seat over 20,000 spectators on the stone terraces. There are more expensive seats in the centre on the pitch. The performance takes place on the Kop or the Stretford End, as it were, with a huge stage providing great potential for magnificent spectacle. The audience assembles early, bringing cushions and refreshments as at a cricket match in England. As dusk falls, there is an unforgettable scene. Each member of the audience lights a tiny candle collected at the turnstile on entering the arena. The thousands of twinkling lights, together with the moon and the stars, provide a magical prelude to the first notes of the music.

On our first visit, there was much excited anticipation amongst the audience. The tenor in *La Bohème* was to be an up-and-coming young singer called Luciano Pavarotti! The next year we had Placido Domingo in *Aida*. All for not much more than a pound a piece. Of course, it will be a lot more now.

But to return belatedly to the road to Orvieto. Most of these hill towns of Tuscany and Umbria were built on commanding sites, but Orvieto's is perhaps the most spectacular of all. It rises up from the surrounding plain on a great mountain of reddish volcanic rock, and its cathedral is also one of the most spectacular in Europe. The cathedral in fact bears more than a family likeness to that of Siena, and was indeed designed by the same architect. It has the same stunning striped marble effect, this time in alternate layers of black and white. Within, there are famous frescoes by Fra Angelico and Signorelli. In these glorious surroundings an organ recital of the music of J.S. Bach that we chanced upon, sounded all the more impressive.

We spent several very pleasant hours just wandering round the narrow, winding streets of the remarkably well-preserved ancient centre of the city, where the greatest of medieval theologians, Thomas Aquinas, was once a student. We were delighted to discover that there was a room available at a most reasonable rate at the Hotel Duomo on the beautiful cathedral square itself. As the night wore on, however, we gradually realised our mistake, as the powerful cathedral bells infuriatingly recorded the passing of every quarter-hour. More infuriatingly still, another church clock nearby regularly chimed in a couple of minutes later. Sleep did not come easily.

We were soon revived, however, by the next day's drive in perfect weather along a wonderfully scenic and totally deserted road to Todi, yet another picturesque hill town, but one with unexpectedly strong views about motorists. Somewhat to our dismay, our Mini was waved by the police on to a parking ground when we were less than halfway up the hill. We were required to complete the journey on a shuttle bus, leaving our car and its luggage behind. However, when we emerged into another gloriously impressive piazza and were able to admire the ancient 'duomo' and the other dignified buildings in the 'centro storico' without the usual incongruous clutter of modern coaches and cars, we had to concede that the city fathers had got the right idea.

So bemused were we by the medieval elegance of the piazza that we evidently forgot our sleepless night at Orvieto, and unthinkingly accepted a room, again at a very reasonable rate, at what appeared to be the only hotel in the cathedral square. Then, of course, we realised that the car and our belongings were back halfway down the hill. So while Rosemary had a leisurely look around the 'duomo', I walked back to the parking ground, and brandishing the hotel reservation, managed to persuade the police in my minimal Italian to allow me to drive back to the cathedral square.

It was certainly well worth the trouble. In the evening we had the most memorable meal of the tour. In the mellow rays of the setting sun we dined and wined superbly, but cheaply, in the open air on the patio of a belvedere with marvellous views over the valley far below. And if the cathedral bells did sound throughout the night, we certainly did not hear them. When we emerged the next morning, it was fascinating to find Todi bathed in brilliant sunshine above a carpet of clouds below.

I should mention, perhaps, at this point, that meals were unexpectedly one of the pleasant experiences of this tour. One takes it for granted, of course, that the standards will be high in country districts of France, but we found that Tuscany and Umbria were not very far behind. In the larger towns the 'ristorante' would frequently offer a very acceptable and cheap 'menu turistico'. In smaller places family-owned 'trattorie' would offer local specialities equally inexpensively. If the budget was really running low, substantial and sustaining meals could be found surprisingly cheaply in a 'pizzeria' or 'tavola calda' with the emphasis on pizza and pasta. At midday we picnicked luxuriously, but still cheaply, with the emphasis generally on luscious Italian fruit, particularly water-melons at almost give-away prices.

Another superb and largely deserted mountain road brought us to Spoleto, where, unlike Todi, we had no difficulty in parking just round the corner from the cathedral. We soon realised that Spoleto is a hill town with a difference. While clearly immensely proud of its well-preserved reminders of earlier civilisations, Etruscan, Roman, medieval, and Renaissance, it also has its feet planted firmly in the present. Every summer Spoleto hosts an internationally renowned 'Festival of Two Worlds' which was founded by the Italian composer Menotti, and which seeks to present the latest creative trends in music and the pictorial arts against the background of its ancient monuments.

So finally to Gubbio, which had been strongly recommended to us by our Italian friends, and which proved to be in many ways the high spot of this most enjoyable tour. Our entry into the town was rather dramatic. The blue skies and brilliant sun that accompanied us throughout our trip abruptly disappeared, lightning flashed, and torrents of water swept down the precipitous lanes that pass for streets in Gubbio.

We hastened to take refuge in the first hotel that we saw. An astonishingly obliging hotel manager braved the deluge to help us manoeuvre on to the only available tiny parking spot. The storm clouds quickly rolled away, however, to be replaced by the glorious sunshine of a late summer evening, which added to our enjoyment of the mellow medieval atmosphere of one of the loveliest of Italian hill towns.

It's sad to have to relate that there was an unfortunate ending to this otherwise idyllic holiday, and one that certainly reinforced our prejudice about motoring in big cities, particularly Italian ones. It came to our notice, while we were in Tuscany, that the famous Shroud of Turin, or 'La Sindona', as the Italians call it, was that very month being given one of its very rare appearances on public display. My historian wife had made a special study of the Shroud, and had given several talks on the subject to interested groups back home. This was for her clearly an opportunity too good to miss.

So we forgot our misgivings about motoring in large cities, and at the end of our tour of Umbria headed for Turin. As we left the motorway on the outskirts of the city we were encouraged to find a special Tourist Information Bureau for the benefit of visitors to the Shroud. A very helpful young lady with excellent English provided us with directions, and advised us to park in a central piazza close by the cathedral, where the Shroud was on display.

We found the parking without difficulty and walked to the nearby 'duomo'. At this point I should explain that all through this tour my wife was hampered by an injured ankle which she had broken some months before, and was walking with the help of a stick. We were confronted by two long queues, one very long, one rather shorter. (This in itself seemed something of a miracle: normally Italians simply do not queue.) A notice informed us that those in the longer queue would be rewarded with a close-up view, but could expect to wait two hours. The shorter queue would involve a wait of only about half an hour, but would be allowed no nearer than 20 yards from the Shroud. Because of my wife's ankle, we settled for the shorter queue. After a few minutes we had a pleasant surprise. A kind steward, observing my wife's difficulties, urgently beckoned us out of the queue, and escorted us to two reserved seats right at the front of the nave, where we had an absolutely first-rate, unimpeded view.

The Holy Shroud was suspended high above in a transparent case, well illuminated so that all the details familiar from reproductions were clearly visible. We were well aware, of course, of the controversy about its authenticity. But as we gazed in awe at this most celebrated of Christian relics, with its remarkable and puzzling 'negative' image, we felt unquestionably in the presence of something uniquely sacred and worthy of veneration.

A few minutes later we came down to earth with a vengeance. The car had been broken into, in broad daylight, in the middle of the afternoon on an official car park. Some villain had smashed the driver's window, and absconded with our main case. Rosemary borrowed a brush and shovel from a nearby shop with which to clear up the worst of the mess of broken glass, while I went in search of the nearest police station. There I stood in yet another queue for at least an hour, while people of various nationalities reported similar disasters.

We should have been making for France that evening by the Mont Cenis Pass, but I didn't fancy the Alps without a driver's window. So after shopping for overnight necessities such as pyjamas and toilet requirements, we booked into another hotel on the outskirts of Turin. The next day there was another minor miracle; I quickly found a garage mechanic who saw no problem at all about replacing the window in the Mini. In fact, rather like the Swiss mechanic at the start of the journey, he seemed positively delighted to be able to help the English visitors, and immediately set to work. When we tried to reward him with a substantial tip for his very prompt service, he said, 'No, no, una cartolina,' and repeated this several times.

Finally the penny dropped. He wanted us to send him a picture postcard to let him know that we had got home safely. Nice chaps, these garage mechanics! We sent him a beautiful picture of the Trough of Bowland; not quite the Alps perhaps, but I'm sure that he would have been pleased.

CHAPTER FOUR

Spain–Catalonia

Before beginning the next two chapters, which tell the story of the best of our wanderings by car around Spain, I feel that I ought to explain in a short preamble how we have been unusually lucky when planning these expeditions to have the expert advice and generous hospitality of the Spanish branch of Rosemary's family. To explain this adequately, I need to take the reader back to that tragic period of Spanish history, the Civil War of 1935-38, which many pensioners with long memories will readily recall.

In recent times most people have been greatly distressed to watch on their televisions the harrowing scenes of savagery in the civil war in the former Yugoslavia. Many pensioners will also remember events no less dreadful in the Spanish Civil War of the 1930s. The great difference, of course, is that television brings these horrific events right into our sitting rooms, whereas in the thirties we could only hear about them on the radio or read about them in the reports of newspaper war correspondents.

In the Spanish Civil War one of the most distinguished of these reporters was Henry Buckley, the war correspondent of the *Daily Telegraph*, and the Martin Bell, as it were, of the Spanish Civil War. Henry was my wife's first cousin and always kept regularly in touch with her. He only narrowly survived the war. There is a family horror story of how Ernest Hemingway, later the celebrated novelist, saved Henry's life at the Battle of the Ebro by rowing him under heavy fire across the river near Tortosa.

Amazingly Henry found an opportunity while covering the war in Catalonia to marry, with full church ceremonial, Maria de Planos, the daughter of the permanent Mayor of Sitges. After the Second World War, Henry became head of Reuter's news agency in Spain. He and Maria settled in Sitges and raised their three sons fluent in three languages, Catalan, Spanish and English.

The eldest of these, Raymond, Ramon in Catalan, spent his university years in his father's home town of Manchester, where he did an honours degree in Spanish. He readily conceded that this occasioned him no great problems. He followed this with an MA degree in English at Madrid University, and a PhD in Spanish at an American university. He is now a professor of Spanish in America, but spends much of his time lecturing to his students in Spain, and conducting them round places of historic and literary importance.

During Raymond's years at Manchester University, he often spent weekends and short holidays at our home in Preston, and thus a link was forged with the next generation of Spanish Buckleys. It was actually Henry Buckley who first suggested to us the idea of an exchange of houses for the holidays. It seemed to us an excellent scheme; he and Maria would have a base from which to visit Henry's many relations in the Lancashire area, while we would have a house in a most attractive resort on the Costa Dorada. The idea was agreed in principle, but never came to pass because of illness.

Unhappily Henry died shortly afterwards, but his widow Maria still kept in touch with Rosemary and pressed us repeatedly to come and stay with her in Sitges. When retirement arrived, the invitation fitted perfectly into our plans. 'You must come for our great fiesta of Corpus Christi,' wrote Maria, so we gratefully accepted.

We already knew from many conversations with Raymond that Sitges is one of the most beautiful and unusual of the Spanish Mediterranean resorts. Although a mere 20 miles south of Barcelona, it has somehow contrived to preserve much of the character and charm of the original fishing village. The modern tower blocks are fewer and less oppressive than in most resorts, and the old town away from the beaches has become something of a centre of Catalan arts. There is a picturesque artists' quarter and a superb small museum.

The feast of Corpus Christi is celebrated with enormous pomp and ceremony in many parts of Catholic Europe, but few places can rival Sitges in the sheer spectacle of the celebration. The Buckleys had often described to us before how the streets of the old town are literally carpeted with flowers during the day, in preparation for the great Corpus Christi Procession of the Blessed Sacrament in the evening.

First we had to get there, however. We decided on a plan that we followed on all our subsequent visits to Spain, namely to treat the journey as an interesting part of the holiday by making a leisurely progress along the minor roads of France and using our favourite small hotels en route, as described in the previous chapters of this book. In this way we eventually arrived at Foix in the foothills of the French Pyrenees, an interesting small town with a picturesque and massive castle. From Foix the plan was to ignore the highways that go round the Pyrenees and to cross the mountains via Andorra, the little independent principality that nestles in the hills between France and Spain. We stopped for petrol in Foix and a chatty garage attendant asked us where we were heading. When we told him he informed us cheerfully that it was snowing in Andorra and the pass would be closed!

So, after an urgent council of war, we decided to forget Andorra and instead make for Perpignan and the motorway round the Costa Brava. To our astonishment we found the 'autopista', the motorway from the Spanish frontier, virtually deserted, and so it continued all the way to the vicinity of Barcelona. Even in this area traffic was never more than thin. We decided that Spanish motorways must be the motorist's dream of heaven. In subsequent years and on other Spanish motorways we have found the situation much the same. In fact, only a few days before writing these words I was travelling again along the same 'autopista' and found the traffic still, in 1993, extremely light, while lorries were thundering down the nearby coastal road. The explanation is apparently complicated and connected with the tolls which are certainly expensive, and the fact that the various sections of the motorway are in different private hands.

So we arrived in Sitges considerably earlier than expected, only to find our hosts gravely embarrassed. They sorrowfully greeted us with the news that their new Catalan regional government, whose installation in Barcelona they had enthusiastically welcomed, had immediately abolished some public holidays, including Corpus Christi. As a result the fiesta had been transferred from the traditional Thursday to the following Sunday.

Fierce discussions in incomprehensible Catalan were raging in the Buckley household and elsewhere. 'They say we must work harder to improve the economy, that we have too many holidays. But to abolish Corpus! They must have gone mad!' So we found ourselves unexpectedly with several spare days. After consultations with Raymond, we decided, on the Thursday that should have been Corpus, to visit Tarragona, the ancient capital of Roman Spain, and on the next day to make a trip into the mountains to the famous Monastery of Montserrat.

Tarragona, the 'City of the Scipios', boasts possibly the finest Roman remains to be found anywhere outside Italy. The historic centre of the city is encircled by enormous walls which the Romans built on existing cyclopean foundations. The blocks of stone are so huge that it is impossible to imagine how they could have been erected without modern mechanical means. Along one section of these walls is a beautifully organised 'paseo arqueologico', a sort of history trail, pleasantly shaded by great cypresses, which presents a series of reminders of Tarragona's illustrious Roman past. These include a laurel grown from a cutting from the Capitol in Rome, a copy of the famous statue on the Capitol of the wolf suckling Romulus and Remus, and finally a statue of the Emperor Augustus presented in 1934 by the city of Rome to her 'daughter Tarragona'. This took me back to my visit to Rome as a schoolboy in the previous year, when Mussolini was clearly hard at work trying to propagate the myth that he was restoring the glories of the Roman Empire.

There is also an extremely well-presented 'Museo Arqueologico' which, in addition to the usual array of statues, pottery and utensils both domestic and agricultural, includes some really superb mosaics, of which the star item is certainly the celebrated 'Head of Medusa', with the remarkable penetrating gaze. I have just one minor criticism of the museum. The individual exhibits are all explained in the native Catalan and one foreign language, Spanish! We have always been puzzled why so many museums in major tourist areas don't encourage their British, and particularly American visitors, with translations in English.

Near one end of the Paseo is the Praetorium or Roman Governor's Palace dating from the first century BC. This is also known locally as the 'Torreon de Pilatos', because of a long-held tradition that Pontius Pilate, the famous or infamous Governor of Judea at the time of Christ, was born here. Whatever the truth of this story, it is apparently historical fact that Pilate's father was governor of Tarraconnensis, and also that another distinguished visitor stayed here, the Emperor Augustus himself.

Prominent in this historic centre of Tarragona, but rather over-shadowed by all the Roman remains, is a very notable medieval cathedral, but like so many Spanish cathedrals somewhat dark and gloomy within. Also like several other Spanish cathedrals it stands on the site of an earlier Moorish mosque, which itself was built where a Roman temple to Jupiter had earlier stood. Perhaps its most attractive feature is the really lovely cloisters adorned with orange trees and rose bushes.

Another notable feature of Tarragona is the 'Balcon del Mediterraneo', a long elevated promenade with fine views over the sea, and a Roman amphitheatre of the Augustan period which was only excavated in 1952. At one point along the 'Balcon' we came across a modern sundial with an intriguing inscription: 'Solem detexi teque sol. Hic si manes Tarraconis urit amor'. After much profound cogitation I offer with misgivings the following transla-tion: 'I have uncovered the sun, and the sun has uncovered you'. (A reference here to the sunbathers?) 'If you linger here, love of Tarragona inflames you.' We certainly agreed with that last senti-ment; Roman Tarragona is an enchanting city.

On our return from Tarragona Raymond indicated that he would be happy to fill in the next day, Friday, by taking us either to Barcelona or to the monastery of Montserrat. It was a difficult choice. We had never been to Barcelona and would have liked in particular to see the 'Sagrada Familia', the architecturally revolutionary church left unfinished by the great architect Antoni Gaudi. However, the monastery of Montserrat we knew was one of the great sights of Europe, and we did not take long to plump for that.

Knowing that his compatriots were notoriously slow to get moving in the morning, Raymond proposed an early start to beat the coachloads of tourists who come in great numbers from the resorts along the coast. On the way he explained that Montserrat in Spanish means the jagged mountain, but that the Catalan name is 'Montsagrat' and means the holy mountain. We climbed 2,377 feet in the 30 odd miles from sea level to monastery, but the journey presented few problems. From the motorway or N11 you take a well-signposted and very steep mountain road with a series of hairpin bends, but all so well engineered that our small car positively scampered to the top. We were at the monastery by 10 am and met not a single coach on the way.

As we emerged in front of the monastery, the scene was quite breathtaking. The monastic buildings themselves are modern and relatively unremarkable, but they seem to be in imminent danger of being crushed beneath the colossal crags that rear up in weird and fantastic shapes immediately above them. One remembers that there has been a monastery on this spot for nearly a thousand years; one just hopes that the giant cliffs will hold up a little longer!

The first monastery is reputed to have been founded as early as AD 880. Its medieval successor was sacked by Napoléon's armies in 1811 and was later abandoned for a time. It was re-occupied in 1860 and the buildings only finally completed this century. Surprisingly, since Catalonia saw some of the fiercest fighting of the Civil War, it survived unscathed.

From the monastery level we ascended another 1,000 feet or so on a funicular railway and got a fascinating close-up of the enormous rocks, with their bizarre configurations, looming immediately above. From this vantage point there is also an absolutely stunning view down over the monastery and the plain beyond to the blue Mediterranean in the far distance. Somewhat unexpectedly at this height there are walkable paths to various hermitages in the hills and, still more surprisingly, a small restaurant at which we enjoyed a lunch of Catalan specialities at a very reasonable price.

Montserrat, with its unique situation, has inevitably attracted a wealth of legend. In the most famous of these it is the resting place of the Holy Grail — a claim which inspired Richard Wagner to make Montserrat the setting for his music-drama *Parsifal*. Another legend centres on the Black Madonna in the monastery chapel which is still revered by thousands of pilgrims every year. According to this legend the statue was the work of St Luke the Evangelist (one of several we have seen in monasteries around Europe). Its discovery in a cave, the 'Santa Cueva', which one can visit, was the reason for the foundation of the monastery in 880.

The unique and spectacular scenery of Montserrat would be reason enough for making the trip from the coast, but there is much else of interest. Visitors are welcome to attend the conventual Mass sung daily in Catalan, and at 1 pm on most days you can listen to the celebrated 'Escalonia', a boys' choir reckoned to be in the same league as the Vienna Boys' Choir.

In modern times this thriving monastery of some 300 monks has been a focal point of the Catalan language and culture. This was never more important than during the fascist regime of Generalissimo Franco. One of the major policies of the dictator was to forge a strong unified Spain, and to this end he sought to suppress the various minority groups, particularly the Basques and Catalans. Throughout the Franco regime it was a criminal offence in Catalonia to use the Catalan language in public. Catalan books were burned, and the language was banned in schools. Shopkeepers were even forbidden to put Catalan names on their goods. Raymond told us that an uncle of his went to gaol for inadvertently using some of his pre-war bill-heads that were printed in Catalan.

Throughout this period, however, the monks of the monastery of Montserrat pursued a policy of sublime passive resistance, and continued to preach and to write in the Catalan language exactly as before. The international prestige of the monastery was such that Franco never seems to have dared to do much about it.

There was one other thing that at Raymond's urgent insistence we did not neglect. In the monastery shop we purchased a couple of bottles of the monks' own Montserrat liqueur. Not so renowned as the Bénédictine or Chartreuse produced by their brethren from other monasteries, it does not seem to appear in commercial wine shops or on supermarket shelves, but it is just as good and far cheaper. It helped to remind us during the cold winter months of one of the most remarkable spots in sunny Spain.

On Saturday preparations were well advanced for the

postponed fiesta on Sunday. We now realised that the famous carpets of flowers were a far more elaborate affair than we had imagined. All through that day and well into the night Maria and her friends were hard at work laboriously plucking petals from the trainload of flowers that had come in from Barcelona. We were happy to be pressed into service. It was early on Saturday evening that things began to go wrong. To the general disbelief the sky clouded over and it began to rain. This was simply unheard of, so the workers ignored the weather and confident that the sun would soon return, continued on their knees in the street to pack the compressed petals tightly together to fill out with colour the intricate designs already sketched lightly on the ground.

On Sunday morning the rain continued, and spectators under umbrellas passed in a steady procession along the pavements to admire the designs, which even in damp and dismal conditions were quite remarkable. As the rain continued, the despondency deepened. Coming from Lancashire, we felt we should be experts on the subject, and offered optimistic suggestions like 'Rain before seven, shine before eleven'. But no such luck; the rain obstinately continued. While the young people packing the petals were still stubbornly and optimistically pressing on with their task, we visited the National Carnation Show which is held annually at Sitges to coincide with the Corpus Christi fiesta. It would probably have been magnificent in the sun, but in the rain it was mildly disappointing and not a patch on the great Southport Flower Show back home, with which we had expected it to compare.

Raymond then took us along to the Cau Ferrat Museum, which really was immensely impressive. The museum is the former home and studio of Santiago Rusinol, one of the founder fathers of modern Catalan painting, who bequeathed the house to the town on his death. It now houses a fine collection of the artist's own work, but also two masterpieces by El Greco, 'St. Mary Magdalen' and 'St. Peter in Tears', and some minor Picasso. Also much art nouveau, ceramics, and *objets d'art* assorted, and if that were not enough, the world's greatest collection of wrought-iron door knockers!

Rusinol was a good friend of Maria's father, the Mayor, and presented him with a couple of his paintings which we had admired on the walls of her house. Maria told us later that she had been asked to lend the pictures for some national exhibition of Spanish painting and had been staggered to find them insured for many millions of pesetas.

It rained all day, and in the evening the Procession of the Blessed Sacrament, that is the culminating high point of the fiesta, and the very *raison d'être* of the carpets of flowers, had to be abandoned. Fierce arguments were raging into the night. Thursday had seen the normal hot sunshine of Sitges in June; on Sunday it had rained all day. The conclusion, it was considered, was inescapable. The unseasonable weather was clearly an act of God and retribution for the government's sacrilegious insult to the great feast of Corpus Christi.

'Never in all my 70 years', wailed Maria, 'has it rained on Corpus before!' But of course it wasn't Corpus. 'You can bet your bottom peseta that Corpus will be back on Thursday next year', said Raymond, with a quiet confidence and a nice mixture of his languages. And so it was! Next year an ecstatic letter from Maria informed us that Corpus had been back on Thursday, its proper date, and that the sun had shone as always before. We must come again!

It was a few years before we could accept this renewed invitation. In the meantime we had successfully used several of the Pyrenean passes on other expeditions. We had driven through Andorra, but disliked the hordes of bargain hunters staggering to their cars carrying TV sets, fridges and the like. We had enjoyed the Somport Pass which was convenient after a visit to Lourdes, and especially the legendary Roncevalles Pass, but that was scarcely on the route to Sitges.

So after spending as usual a few days on our favourite minor roads of France, we opted for the route which initially is the road to Andorra, but then skirts the principality, and proceeds to Spain through Bourg Madame. The big notice at the foot of the pass said 'Ouvert', meaning presumably not blocked by snow, which was a relief after our earlier experience. There was no mention of fog.

So off we went, cheerfully all unsuspecting, and had just got beyond the point of no return when visibility was suddenly reduced to 10 yards or less in an impenetrable fog. It was the only really frightening experience I have had in driving tens of thousands of miles all over the Continent. The fog was soon so bad that I had no points of reference whatsoever to keep us safely clear of the precipices below. However, Rosemary in the passenger seat, and therefore in our English car with its right-hand drive near the centre of the road, could just discern the white line along the middle of the road. I actually drove for half an hour or so following her instructions, 'Now gradually round to the right, now straighten up again!' In this extraordinary manner we negotiated the innumerable 'virages' or hairpin bends on the road up the pass. Our relief can be imagined when quite suddenly we emerged into brilliant Spanish sunshine and the road ahead was clear.

Despite this poor start, we arrived in Sitges on time to lend a hand again with the plucking of the petals from the trainload of flowers, the first stage in the creation of the carpets that went on through most of Wednesday night. In the morning we again watched the young people on their knees in the road patiently packing the petals into the colourful and highly artistic designs which had previously been prepared. Not all the designs, we noticed, were entirely liturgical; one design actually featured the Olympic logo, and was pressing the claims of Barcelona to hold the 1992 Olympic Games!

Soon long queues of fascinated sightseers were slowly filing along the narrow pavement admiring the results. Their numbers grew steadily, till by late afternoon the carpeted streets of the old town were largely impassable. In the evening the lovely old church which dominates the town from an elevated position was packed to overflowing for the solemn Mass which precedes the Corpus Christi procession. We were relieved that the sermon in incomprehensible Catalan was mercifully brief.

The balcony of Maria's house in the main street, the Calle Maior, provided an excellent vantage point for watching the procession. It was a strange mixture of the sacred and the secular. Recent first communicants bearing still more flowers escorted the priest carrying the Blessed Sacrament. Somewhat incongruously the procession was led by the 'Giants', those towering puppets which

seem to be an essential part of any Spanish fiesta, religious or secular. A band mainly composed of Catalan shaums, a sort of primitive oboe, played raucous music that was anything but ecclesiastical.

The next day, when the excitement had died down, we enjoyed a quiet stroll along the Paseo Maritimo, the long promenade with shady palm trees which, though quiet and peaceful in late spring, we knew would be seething with holidaymakers in only a few weeks' time. We were intrigued to discover at one point on the Paseo, that there was someone else who also loved Sitges in the spring. Much to our surprise we came across a memorial to G.K. Chesterton, the distinguished English writer of the earlier part of the century. A stone slab, complete with an excellent portrait, has an inscription which, literally translated, reads 'To G.K. Chesterton, Lover of Sitges, Who honoured her Springs with his noble Presence'.

Rosemary was particularly pleased, since she well remembered helping to organise a lecture by the great writer in Manchester in the thirties. On our return to Calle Maior, we mentioned our discovery to Maria. 'Oh yes', she said, 'I remember when I was a young girl seeing him many times sitting in the sunshine, reading or writing'. Then after a pause, she added with a wry smile, 'I suppose he was our first tourist'.

The next day we said our fond farewells and set off for another part of Spain. On the way we paid a brief visit to another famous Catalan monastery, that of Santa Creus. Though certainly not as spectacular as the incomparable Montserrat, Santa Creus is still an impressive sight as one approaches along a minor road from the coast. This great twelfth century church contains the royal tombs of the kings of Aragon, and is plain and austere in the Cistercian tradition. The cloisters are particularly attractive with much rich tracery and a garden full of orange trees. The entrance fee was 200 pesetas, about a pound, but only half of that for 'jubilados', the pleasant Spanish word for OAPs.

At the beginning of this chapter I drew some sad parallels between the civil war in the former Yugoslavia and the Spanish Civil War of the late thirties. I cannot resist a short postscript on the same subject.

It is greatly encouraging to observe the present peaceful and apparently stable political situation in Catalonia, highlighted on the world stage during the Olympic Games in Barcelona. Perhaps the Catalans have something to teach the warring tribes of former Yugoslavia, who seem to be obsessed with grievances stemming from events of 50 years ago and beyond. The Catalans suffered equally grievously under Franco's fascists during their civil war and long after. Helped no doubt by the wise policies of devolution pursued by the king and the post-Franco governments, they seem to be prepared to forgive and forget, to put the past behind them and to concentrate on forging a prosperous future for themselves and their children.

The Pilgrim Madonna, Pontevedra, Spain

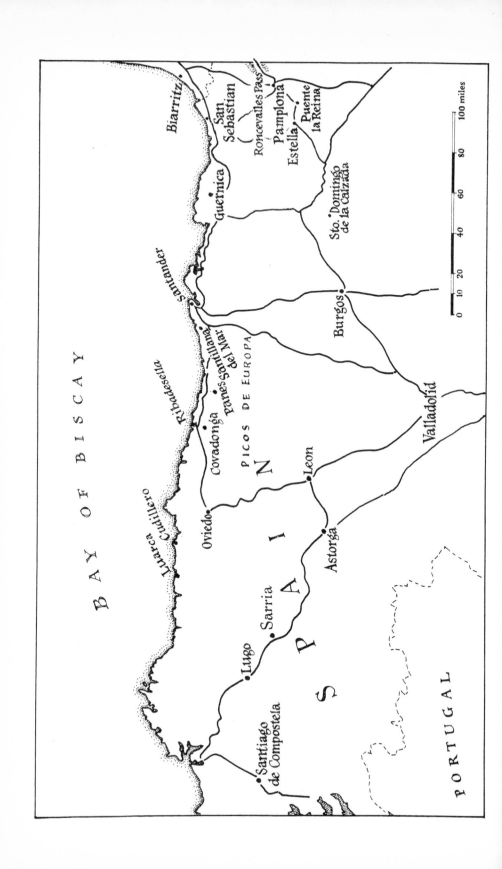

BAY OF BISCAY

Biarritz
San Sebastian
Roncevalles Pass
Pamplona
Puente la Reina
Estella
Guernica
Sto. Domingo de la Calzada
Santander
Ribadesella
Luarca
Cudillero
Panes
Santillana del Mar
Picos DE EUROPA
Covadonga
Burgos
Oviedo
Leon
Valladolid
Astorga
Lugo
Sarria
S P A I N
Santiago de Compostela
PORTUGAL

100 miles
80
60
40
20
0 10

CHAPTER FIVE

Spain–Camino de Santiago

Right from the start of our retirement travels around Europe we had our sights set on some day following the historic 'Camino de Santiago', the medieval pilgrimage route to Santiago de Compostela on the west coast of Spain. Rosemary, of course, was particularly keen; she had always been fascinated by the fact that in the Middle Ages, her special interest, as many as two million dedicated pilgrims each year made the arduous journey across Europe on foot, or occasionally on horseback. If they could do it on foot, surely we could do it in an Austin Metro?

We hesitated at first because of the sheer distance involved — the length of England and France and the breadth of Spain. We would need a longer period of time than we had allotted to our earlier trips, and although retired, we still had minor commitments at home. Cousin Raymond, himself an enthusiast, had been urging us to get on with it for years, as had Marian Curd, the travel editor of *The Universe*, who, incidentally, after our return from Compostela, published four articles by me on our experiences.

Our earlier visit to Rocamadour in the Dordogne, mentioned as a digression in my chapter on Provence, had certainly stimulated our interest, since it was used as a major staging post by thousands of pilgrims coming from England and Ireland. Even more stimulating was the remote Abbey of Conques, which we came upon near the valley of the River Lot, and which was used, like Rocamadour, by pilgrims coming from the east of France, and from Germany and beyond.

The Abbey of Conques is itself a quite remarkable sight, and is claimed to be 'the most audacious abbey building in France' because of its immense height. Even more remarkable is the abbey's 'trésor', which actually figures in the *Guinness Book of Records*, where it is rated 'the most beautiful treasure in France'! This is perhaps not too surprising, since the treasure includes votive offerings from such distinguished visitors as Pepin the Short and the Emperor Charlemagne himself. At Conques we even ventured a few hundred yards on foot along the 'Rue St Jacques', and tried to imagine the feelings of those intrepid foot-sloggers as they faced the prospect of at least another 1,000 kilometres, including the crossing of the Pyrenees.

The final spur to our determination to tackle the 'camino' came at Puente la Reina, where we stopped overnight when returning from a holiday in another part of Spain. There we gazed at the steep medieval bridge which those millions of pilgrims from all parts of Europe had passed across over the centuries. I took a photograph of Rosemary on the historic bridge, and we decided there and then that we would 'do' the 'camino' next year.

This then is perhaps the right moment to consider what on earth could have motivated all those millions to make the arduous journey in the difficult and dangerous conditions of the times. Is there really any firm evidence that St James the Apostle is buried in the cathedral at Compostela, or that he even came to Spain at all? We put the question to cousin Raymond, the learned professor, who replied that he had been asked that question hundreds of times by his students, and had to reply that there simply was no proof, and that indeed the whole story seemed highly improbable. On the other hand, he fully agreed with Rosemary that when a tradition has been so firmly established and revered over so many centuries, it is rash and unscholarly to dismiss it out of hand.

Raymond also urged that we would want to follow the authentic historic 'camino', and avoid the short cuts along modern highways taken by the coach operators. To this end he kindly supplied us with a detailed itinerary and advice on interesting things to watch out for which we would probably otherwise have missed.

We set off at last on the journey across France, using our favourite and familiar minor roads and small country hotels. The journey was smooth and uneventful all the way to St Jean Pied de Port, at the foot of the Roncevalles Pass. We had naturally not forgotten our frightening experience in dense fog on a Pyrenean pass a few years before, and so were pleased to see the early morning mist rapidly clearing. The road up the pass was astonishingly free of traffic; we met only three lorries and a group of cheerful veteran cyclists.

On arrival at the summit, we were at first distracted from the purpose of our trip by an unexpected war memorial commemorating not the two world wars, but the battle of AD 778, in which the rearguard of Charlemagne's army, commanded by Roland and Oliver, was ambushed and destroyed by the Moors, or more probably, according to some recent research, by the Basques. The story is told in the famous medieval epic, *Le Chanson de Roland*. Charlemagne was definitely one of Rosemary's favourite historical figures, so I dutifully took her photograph again alongside the monument.

The other point of interest at the top of the pass that most definitely brought us back to the business in hand, was a signpost pointing the road down into Spain. Instead of indicating the distance to Pamplona, the nearest large town on the way, it said 'Santiago 789 kilometres', and above was a cockle shell, the symbol of the 'camino', the same cockle shell that we were to find marking the authentic route the whole of those 789 kilometres.

A short distance along the road we came to Roncevalles Abbey, an Augustinian foundation of the twelfth century. This vast, rather sombre building, rich in relics of both Charlemagne and the pilgrims of the 'camino', was the first of many monasteries and hospices that we were to encounter along the route that offered succour and hospitality to weary pilgrims. We could readily imagine them, exhausted after that punishing climb to the top of the pass, thankfully staggering into this haven of rest and refreshment.

We shunned the modern highway to Pamplona and followed instead a minor road through superb Pyrenean scenery to the little village of Aoiz. Here we found a lovely Romanesque church and a Roman bridge, still surprisingly coping with traffic of the twentieth century. We entered the church, which was disappointingly dark, until a kindly sacristan pottering around in the gloom insisted on floodlighting for our inspection a superb golden, baroque altarpiece. This was the first of many such churches of unexpected magnificence that we came across on our way. Presumably, like Rocamadour and Conques, these churches were the fortunate beneficiaries of the generosity of passing pilgrims of the wealthier kind.

A little further along the road and we were back in Puente la Reina, which had clinched last year our decision to undertake the pilgrimage. On the edge of the village, at the point where our road joined that from Pamplona, there stood a fine modern statue of a medieval pilgrim in the traditional garb of wide-brimmed hat with cockle shell badge, long cape and staff. Beneath the statue was an inscription: 'Y desde aqui todos los caminos a Santiago se hagen uno solo' — 'From this point all roads to Santiago are one'. Though not quite, as we were to discover later.

That single road then goes through the middle of the little town past two notable churches and a hospice, all dating from the great days of the 'camino'. In one of these churches is a much revered Y-shaped crucifix on which Christ is depicted with a wonderfully expressive face. This heavy wooden crucifix was actually carried from Germany by a pilgrim in the fourteenth century. He had clearly intended carrying it to Compostela, but had given up the unequal struggle at Puente. The other church contains an impressive wooden statue of St James the Pilgrim, depicting the saint barefoot and in the traditional pilgrim's costume. The wall behind the altar in this Church of St James is again a mass of gold from roof to floor.

The little town of today clearly has no wish to capitalise on its historic past. There is no commercialisation whatsoever, no souvenir shops selling picture postcards and, as far as we could see, only one hotel. There we had a room with shower and private loo for approximately £10, and a meal of 'sopa di pescado', pork chop and chips, and strawberries and cream for £5, with a bottle of wine included. This proved to be about the going rate for the rest of the tour.

At Estella la Bella our contemplation of the impressive Church of San Pedro de la Rua with a notable Moorish façade was rudely disturbed by a boisterous party of Spanish school-children. As former members of the teaching profession, we have often noted with admiration how Spanish teachers seem happy to take large parties of pupils on educational trips to the most surprising venues. However, we have also sometimes been dismayed by the way they then allow them to riot all over the place. This lot had spotted the GB plate on our car and were eager to seize the opportunity to try out the English they were learning at school. While their teachers smiled indulgently, they more or less hemmed us in, and bombarded us with questions about ourselves, our family, our town, and, of course, the terrible English weather.

Escaping at last, we pressed on to Santo Domingo de la Calzada, which owes its name to an eleventh century hermit who is credited with having built a bridge here for the benefit of the pilgrims. It is the town's cathedral, however, which is the main centre of interest today, and for a very odd reason. As we entered the cathedral we were greeted by a most un-ecclesiastical sound, a loud cock-crow which echoed eerily round the building. We then saw that high up in the Gothic splendour of a transept was a hen coop, housing a cock and hen.

This bizarre arrangement commemorates a popular legend dating back once more to the hey-day of the 'camino'. According to this, a pilgrim was falsely accused of a grievous crime by a lady of easy virtue whose advances he had spurned. He was condemned to death, but his fellow pilgrims were so incensed that they pursued the magistrate to his home, and found him about to lunch on a roast chicken. But the magistrate was adamant. 'He shall hang', he said, 'unless that chicken gets up and crows'. Which, of course, the bird obligingly did.

We were wondering how the poultry were enjoying their unusual lodgings, and remembering that the Spaniards are less sensitive, to say the least, about animal rights than we are, wondered also what the RSPCA might think about it all. Whereupon the cock, as if to reassure us about the health and happiness of himself and partner, produced an ear-splitting repeat performance of his cock-a doodle-doo.

By a happy chance, two of the finest cathedrals in Spain, and indeed in the whole of Europe, those of Burgos and Leon, are on the route to Compostela. We had visited Burgos once before, and had found the interior of the cathedral disappointingly dark. A huge stone screen prevents any view down the nave, and the notable side-chapels are blocked off by the inevitable Spanish wrought-iron gates. But this time we were in luck. Two of the finest showpieces of the cathedral were suddenly floodlit for the benefit of a French guided party. So we were able to admire, at the Frenchmen's expense, the celebrated golden staircase which, smothered in rich Renaissance ornamentation, rises in the shape of a diamond to the great north door.

Similarly illuminated for the benefit of the French was the magnificent octagonal lantern, which, on massive piers, rises to a tremendous height in the centre of the nave above the tomb of the legendary hero El Cid. We were strolling around the cathedral, admiring these and the many other wonders of this superb building when we were unbelievably greeted by one of my past pupils and his brother and sister-in-law who, like us, were awaiting the start of the Sunday High Mass. There was inevitably much reference to the old cliché 'It's a small world'.

Of all the places on the road to Compostela, Burgos is perhaps the one that most merits some time for lingering and leisurely inspection, since it has been at the centre of Spanish history from El Cid to Generalissimo Franco. Since it was Sunday, we had found a parking space without difficulty right in the centre of the city. On this occasion, of course, it just happened that we were in Burgos on Sunday, but in all our travels around Europe experience has taught us that Sunday is much the best day of the week for exploring the sights of major cities. The traffic is generally negligible, the streets are peaceful and quiet, and parking in the centre is usually permissible all day and free of charge.

So we took advantage of our central parking to see some of the other sights when we left the cathedral. Not far away is a hugely impressive gateway, the Arco de Santa Maria, flanked by tall semi-circular towers and featuring on its front statues of famous figures in the city's long history, inevitably including El Cid. The Cid, of course, also has a statue to himself which, as we approached it from a distance, looked like a great black bat against the sky.

Perhaps the most interesting building in Burgos, apart from the cathedral, is the beautifully restored fifteenth century Casa del

Cordon, so-called because of a Franciscan girdle motif which decorates the façade. A large inscription in Spanish on the front wall of the house tells how the Catholic monarchs, Ferdinand and Isabella, in this house on 23 April 1497 graciously received Christopher Columbus on his return from his second voyage to the New World, and 'confirmed all his privileges'.

However, it was none of these historic monuments that was our favourite and abiding memory of Burgos, but rather a charming little scene that we happened upon by chance in the tiny Church of San Nicolas, which is almost alongside the cathedral. The church is renowned for its remarkable alabaster altar-piece of 1505 by Simon of Cologne, but we had to delay our inspection of this till the end of a picturesque and typically Spanish baptismal ceremony. The actual christening was just ending as we entered. Thereupon two very small children in picturesque traditional costume, presumably members of the family, solemnly performed a 'sarabande' or similar stately dance to the accompaniment of primitive music on tape. This was followed by much chaotic photography of family parties grouped around the newly-born.

Between the cathedral cities of Burgos and Leon there was little of note except some diabolically bad main roads and some fairly dreary scenery. Hotels, too, were very few and far between, but we found one just in the nick of time at Sahagun. We thought ourselves lucky to get a room as there was clearly some minor fiesta taking place, with bands and bunting and, of course, a bullfight. Because of the bullfight we were told not to expect a meal before 10 pm at the earliest. And no sleep till the early hours, as the noise and excitement continued unabated.

Nevertheless we were off early next morning for the short drive to Leon. Burgos Cathedral we had found disappointingly dark; Leon could scarcely be a greater contrast. Nowhere in Europe have we seen a cathedral with such a magnificent expanse of colourful, medieval stained glass. When the sun shone, the cathedral seemed bathed in all-glorious technicolour.

Raymond had warned us not to be so overcome by the unique beauties of the cathedral as to overlook another place of compelling interest in Leon, the Royal Pantheon, attached to the Basilica of St

Isidor, which is reputed to contain some of the finest Romanesque frescoes to have survived anywhere in Europe. We were baffled to find the building firmly closed. One of the beggars in the doorway, who unhappily still disfigure the Spanish scene, cried out to us repeatedly, 'Manana, manana', until the penny dropped, and we realised that it was Monday, when most state-run museums, galleries etc. in Spain are closed. We felt that we should reward the poor beggar with a few pesetas.

However, we could not take his advice and return tomorrow, because we were on a pretty tight schedule designed to have us reach Compostela by the feast of Corpus Christi. We did make time, nevertheless, to visit very briefly a striking modern church right on our road, as indicated by its name, La Virgen del Camino, with an immensely tall campanile for so small a church, and 13 great statues of Our Lady and the Twelve Apostles on the façade. The sculptor is one of those now engaged on the task of completing Gaudi's celebrated 'Sagrada Familia' in Barcelona, which became familiar to millions on television as the symbol of Barcelona during the Olympic Games.

Astorga, the next stop on our way, rather resembled a bomb site, with all its roads and pavements apparently under repair at the same time. This seems to be something of a Spanish custom. Even main roads are not repaired in short sections as with us, but a start to repairs is made by removing the top surface for up to 10 kilometres at a time. Happily the ancient cathedral and the modern bishop's palace, another Gaudi masterpiece, were still accessible.

Gaudi's extravaganza, a notable example of eccentric neo-Gothic, rather puts the cathedral in the shade. Inside it now houses the 'Museo del Camino' for which there is a small entrance fee, and which contains a remarkable collection of memorabilia from the many centuries of the 'camino', such as ancient maps and documents and dozens of statues and pictures of pilgrims of various periods and, of course, of St James himself. It is Gaudi's extraordinary creation, however, both strange and beautiful, with its equally striking interior decoration, that stays in the memory.

From Astorga the road was surprisingly good but the weather terrible, so we pressed on through Ponferrada without stopping to find a famous castle, and on past Villafranca to Piedrafita, where we had to make an important decision. It was tempting to follow the main road to Lugo and thence on to Compostela. However, Raymond had assured us that the authentic 'camino' from this point followed a minor road through the mountains. We embarked on this with some trepidation, since some supposedly major roads had been bad enough.

It proved to be excellent advice. We were rewarded with a perfectly reasonable, if narrow road through some superb mountain scenery, past the quaint village of El Cebrero, one of the few Celtic villages with thatched roofs still surviving in Spain. Raymond's confidence about the genuine 'camino' was vindicated by a succession of signposts adorned with a cockle shell, and even in one instance a signpost in the form of a pilgrim in traditional dress.

Now we were on the last leg, through Samos, Sarria and Puertomarin to Labacolla. Our passage through Sarria was enlivened by a ludicrous episode in a bank. Here I presented an American Express Traveller's cheque for £100, which surely should have caused no problems. The young bank clerk viewed it with great suspicion, however, and hesitated some time before deciding that it was safe to cash it. He then did a little sum on a piece of paper. The exchange rate at the time was about 205 pesetas to the pound, so I made a mental note that I should expect to receive about 20,500 pesetas.

The bank clerk then gave a stunning display of professional expertise, counting the notes at dazzling speed. I observed that there seemed to be an awful lot of them, and presumed that they must be of a very small denomination. The conjuring trick completed, he stuck the package into my hand and wished me a cheery 'Adios'. I then took a seat at the back of the bank, in order to stuff the wad safely into my wallet. Gradually, however, the feeling grew upon me that something was wrong. I easily become confused with all those noughts at the end of lire and pesetas; equally, I naively presume that bank clerks are mathematically infallible.

However, the conclusion gradually became inescapable that this generous fellow had given me not £100, but £1,000 in exchange for my £100 cheque! The next problem was how in my minimal Spanish to explain to him that he had perpetrated a colossal professional boob. I pondered this for a few minutes, but I needn't have bothered. Suddenly an agitated bank clerk shot across the bank like the proverbial scalded cat, and violently snatched the whole package out of my hand.

He then angrily summoned me back to his counter and did his little sum again, laboriously multiplying 100 by 205. It didn't seem to occur him just to add two noughts to 205. Having secured my agreement to the answer, he then repeated the conjuring trick, but this time with notes of the right denomination. He again wished me a cordial 'Adios' and seemed in no way embarrassed or abashed. In fact, he contrived somehow to imply that it was, of course, all my stupid fault.

I have often wondered what would have happened if I had unwittingly gone straight out of the bank to the car without checking the pesetas. I suppose I might have ended up in a Spanish gaol since, of course, the bank clerk had all my personal particulars from my passport. Actually, this strange episode encouraged me to abandon travellers' cheques for subsequent excursions abroad. I have found that I can manage perfectly well with a small amount of currency for minor expenses, plus a Visa credit card, which is now universally accepted everywhere in Europe.

At Labacolla, if we had followed faithfully the example of the medieval pilgrims, we should have climbed a nearby small hill, and cheered enthusiastically at the first sight of the towers of Compostela. Pilgrims also used to wash here to remove the grime of the journey and approach the holy city in a seemly state. We decided to postpone these ablutions till we had safely lodged ourselves inside an hotel in Compostela.

Finding an hotel presented no difficulty at all, and we secured a double room with private bath and loo at the Hotel Restaurante Barbante in the Calle Franco for 3,000 pesetas (£15). For an hotel in a prestige position, only a stone's throw from the cathedral, we thought this reasonable indeed. Parking was not quite so simple, however. The hotel manager cheerfully suggested that we leave the car where it was just outside the hotel — until I spotted a jolly little notice indicating that cars so parked would be towed away by crane! Fortunately we found legal parking not far away behind the 'correos', the GPO.

As we relaxed at last over a drink in the lounge, our sense of achievement at having arrived safely at Compostela bang on target for the great feast of Corpus Christi on the morrow was, quite unreasonably, probably as great as that of those heroic pedestrian pilgrims of earlier times.

It has been said by Jan Morris, one of the most eloquent and perceptive writers on Spain, that to emerge for the first time from the Calle Franco into the vast cathedral square is to experience one of the great moments of travel. The Plaza del Obradoiro, or, as it is sometimes known, the Plaza de España, could easily have degenerated into one gigantic car park. Wisely it has been kept traffic-free, so that one can quietly admire, with unobstructed view, the magnificent buildings that surround it.

We first gazed in awe at the immense baroque façade which has dominated the square since 1750, and which conceals and protects from the weather the earlier Romanesque cathedral behind. Appropriately a statue of St James commands the central gable, flanked by two intricately decorated towers which soar to a height of almost 250 feet. Cousin Raymond, our mentor on this expedition, had insisted that whether we regarded ourselves as pilgrims or mere tourists, we would surely wish to follow the centuries-old ritual observed by all visiting the holy city for the first time.

So, in accordance with his directions, we climbed the great flight of steps from the plaza and entered the cathedral by the majestic Portico de Gloria, universally acknowledged as one of the supreme masterpieces of medieval art. We decided that it deserved a more leisurely contemplation at a later stage. As the next move in this ritual, we put our hands at the feet of the statue of Christ, and touched our heads gently against the 'pillar of wisdom', the figure of himself that Mateo, the master sculptor, placed at the base of the composition. (In retrospect it is clear that something went wrong at this point, since according to the tradition, a little of his talent should have rubbed off on to us.)

Then into the vast interior to stand in wonderment and awe before the astonishing high altar, a supreme *tour de force* of baroque imagination and ingenuity. Inevitably another statue of St

James is the central feature, richly adorned with gold, silver and precious stones. Figures of pilgrims in their traditional garb are everywhere; there is even a pilgrim placed on top of each of the two pulpits. At a higher level there is yet another statue of the apostle, this time on horseback fiercely brandishing a sword. This relates to the legend that during the 'reconquista', the struggle to recover Spain from Moorish domination, St James himself appeared on a charger beating back the infidels.

Our next move was to descend the steps down into the crypt beneath the high altar to venerate the tomb of the apostle, whose remains are contained in a silver casket along with those of his disciples, Saints Theodore and Athanasius. Finally, we completed this time-honoured ritual by climbing the steps behind the high altar and leaning forward to embrace the statue of the saint by placing our arms gently round his neck. There was no embarrassment whatsoever in performing all this strange ritual; we were merely members of a long queue of people all doing the same thing.

Having therefore fulfilled Raymond's instructions to the letter, we next embarked on a more leisurely tour of this remarkable building, beginning with that stupendous Portico de Gloria at the main entrance. This twelfth century Romanesque masterpiece, rivalled only by the pediments of the French cathedrals of Vezelay and Autun, is in the form of a tripartite porch which tells the story of the Last Judgement, and has been described as itself a veritable museum of Romanesque art. It was carved between AD 1166 and 1188 by the master mason Mateo who, as we have already observed, modestly signed his composition with a kneeling portrait of himself.

The sheer magnificence of the Portico de Gloria could easily make one overlook the other fine doorways, of which we found the Puerta de las Platerias on the south side almost equally impressive. Another unique feature of this remarkable cathedral is that, unlike many other famous cathedrals hemmed in by a clutter of lesser buildings, it can be peacefully and conveniently contemplated and photographed from spacious plazas on every side.

There are other majestic buildings all around the square, of which one is of particular elegance and historic interest. This is the Hostal de los Reyes Catolicos, which as the name indicates, was

SITGES: ARTISTS' QUARTER (Ch. 4) – ABOVE
SITGES: CORPUS CHRISTI (Ch. 4) – BELOW LEFT
MONTSERRAT: MONASTERY (Ch. 4) – BELOW RIGHT

founded by Ferdinand and Isabella. They intended it as a free refuge and hospital for weary and shattered pilgrims arriving after their punishing journey across Europe. It is rather sad to find that it is now ironically a luxury hotel, no doubt one of the most beautiful, but also one of the most expensive in Spain. However, it costs nothing to admire from the plaza the superb plateresque doorway which is intricately carved with coats of arms to the full height of the building. Non-residents can also join a guided tour to inspect some parts of the interior, especially the four internal courtyards and a chapel in the centre with exquisitely carved supporting columns.

On the Feast of Corpus Christi we arrived at the cathedral by half past six for the High Mass at seven o'clock in the evening. We were astounded to discover this vast building already packed to the doors. As we were gazing around disconsolately, a gallant old gentleman insisted on giving Rosemary his seat and propped himself up against a pillar. I could only follow his example. Remembering our experiences in Sitges and other parts of Spain on Corpus Christi, we had presumed that this High Mass and the subsequent procession would be similarly spectacular.

In particular we had expected that there would be a performance by the celebrated 'botafumeiro', the giant censer, which on great feast days is hoisted on pulleys by a team of six men, and swung across the cathedral transept. This is a spectacle which is absolutely unique to Compostela, and which Raymond had described to us in graphic detail. However, for whatever reason, no botafumeiro put in an appearance, and we had to content ourselves with later gazing at the six foot tall censer in the library where it is normally housed. The Corpus Christi procession which later wound round the cathedral squares was notable only for the great numbers participating and was curiously lacking in the spectacle of some other places. Understandably, of course, the great day in Compostela is 25 July, the feast of St James, when flowers, fireworks *and* botafumeiro are positively guaranteed.

We were favoured with fine, sunny weather during our stay in Santiago de Compostela. That statement is not an exercise in the obvious, because it must not be forgotten that Compostela is near the Atlantic, not the Mediterranean, coast of Spain, and is, in fact, one of the wetter cities of Europe. The statistics show that its annual rainfall is approximately equal to that of Manchester! The natives actually refer to the rain affectionately as St James's soup. So we were not surprised when, on the morning of our departure, the heavens opened, and loading the car, parked inconveniently at a distance, had to be managed under an umbrella.

We knew that we had better be prepared for more of the same, since we had planned for the first part of our return journey to drive along Spain's north Atlantic coast, the Costa Verde. When the tourist explosion occurred in Spain with the arrival of cheap air travel, the publicity people thought it would be a good idea if all Spain's coasts had nice descriptive names like the traditional Costa Brava. These, of course, would emphasise their greatest attraction, the sun. So we got Costa del Sol, Costa Dorada, Costa del Luz and the rest. However, they had to think of something different for the frequently cloudy and rainy coasts of Cantabria and Asturias. So they came up with the Costa Verde or the Verdant Coast, designed to reflect appealingly the green pastures and luxuriant vegetation of this north Atlantic region.

We reached the Costa Verde at Luarca early one Sunday morning. This proved a delightful introduction since, in complete peace and quiet, we were able to wander around this pleasant little town with white houses high on a cliff overlooking the picturesque little fishing harbour below. It was very different in the afternoon at Cudillero, an even more picturesque village surrounded by steep cliffs, and often compared in the guide books with Cornish Clovelly or St Ives. As with them on a sunny summer afternoon, it was crowded with day trippers enjoying the sea, the sand and the scenery.

After some tricky navigating by Rosemary, necessary to avoid the big industrial cities of Oviedo and Gijon, we were back at the coast at Ribadesella, where we found a great expanse of beach, on both sides of an estuary, totally deserted. It was the same again at Nueva, which claims to be the most beautiful village in Asturias, and supports its claim by placing plants and flowers in every conceivable spot. Here, the narrow beach, hemmed in by giant cliffs, was again utterly quiet and deserted. This seemed quite astonishing to us in late June, but we were assured that things would be very different in the next two holiday months, when the beaches would be thronged with Spaniards who flock to the Costa Verde in their thousands — to get away from the sun!

From this point we had decided to take the opportunity of a digression into the little-known mountains, the Picos de Europa, a huge range rising in places to nearly 9,000 feet. There's something of a mystery about the curious name of these mountains. The most persuasive theory seems to be that sailors returning home from the early expeditions to the New World, and anxiously scanning the horizon for signs of land, would spot these 'peaks of Europe' on the west coast of Spain as their first glimpse of their homeland.

Equally mysterious is the relative neglect by tourists and the tourist trade of this marvellous mountain scenery. Rosemary and I had already seen much of the Pyrenees, of course, in our travels around France and Spain, and in pre-retirement days we spent two long holidays in the incomparable Italian Dolomites. As we drove along the road from the coast towards the old town of Cangas de Onis, we were soon of the firm opinion that the Picos are scenically no less spectacular.

This impression grew stronger as we climbed a little higher to Covadonga, which is regarded by the Spaniards as something of a national shrine. Here, according to tradition, Pelayo, a local tribal leader, in the year 718 inflicted the first defeat on the Moorish occupiers of the peninsula, and thus began the 'reconquista', the recapture of Spain from the infidels, which was only completed under Ferdinand and Isabella nearly 800 years later.

Covadonga is dominated by a large nineteenth century basilica built in the neo-Romanesque style. On a sort of promenade in front there stands a fine bronze statue of Pelayo himself, brandishing the Cross of Victory that he is said to have carried into battle. Pelayo is buried in the nearby Santa Cueva, reached from the basilica along a short rocky gallery. Also in the cave is the much venerated statue of the Virgin of Covadonga, the centre of a great pilgrimage each September. In a small museum attached to the basilica we noticed, prominently and proudly presented, a letter to Covadonga from Pope John XXIII in which he wrote, 'I love the Madonna of Covadonga as you Asturians love her. I keep her image in my bedroom, and before her I make my first prayer of the day.'

By sheer good luck we happened to arrive at the Santa Cueva along that dark slippery gallery from the basilica just as Mass was beginning at the altar immediately below the famous statue. The cave is half open to the elements and it was raining hard, with heavy clouds gathering all around. The words of the priest were half drowned by the noise of a waterfall cascading down the hillside. Birds flew in and out of the cave during the service, and pigeons perched above the altar. It was yet another of the many unexpected but memorable experiences of this holiday.

The rain mercifully cleared and we took the road for Panes along a lush valley with superb scenery that improved with every mile, so much so that when we happened upon an attractive-looking hotel in a village in the midst of this scenic paradise, we simply couldn't resist it, and booked in for the night. We got a room at the front of the small hotel overlooking the mountains, whose beauty was enhanced by fluffy, cottonwool clouds clinging to the topmost peaks. In addition to the view we had a private bath and loo for 2,000 pesetas and a quite elegant meal for 750 pesetas, including a bottle of wine.

Perhaps this is a good moment to mention that those prices were about par for the course in this mountainous region and right the length of the Costa Verde. Cheap but perfectly adequate accommodation was plentiful everywhere we went. The magic word to look out for was 'habitaciones', the Spanish equivalent of French 'chambres' and German 'zimmer'. They were provided not only by pleasant small hotels, but also over many restaurants and 'fondas' (pubs), and even in private houses. The quality of the meals was generally surprisingly high, if not quite up to French standards, and there was almost always a bottle of 'vino tinto' included.

Everything about that small hotel at Ortiguero was so splendid, the accommodation, the cuisine, and above all, the stunning views, that we opted for a second night and a day's relaxation in between. Next day the road to Panes became steadily narrower and more tortuous. From Panes we were planning to follow the 'Hermida Defile' to Potes, a route to which Michelin accords his rare accolade of three asterisks. However, we were slightly intimidated by his further remark, 'The gorge is narrow and so dim as to be bare of vegetation; the River Deva has sought out weaknesses in the rock wall so that its course swings like a pendulum.'

Panes, unexpectedly for so small a place, boasted a 'Turismo', a Tourist Information Office. An obliging young lady behind the counter surprisingly had no English, and less surprisingly, could not follow my Spanish. So we settled for French, and she was most reassuring that the road to Potes was 'pas difficile'. Thus encouraged, we pressed on through scenery that was by now quite sensational. Happily the weather, initially dull, became gloriously sunny, and helped to convince us that these Picos de Europa, some still under snow, were the equal of the best of the Italian Dolomites.

A short distance beyond Potes we reached the monastery of Santo Toribio de Liebana. Rosemary had often remarked during our travels in various countries how the medieval monks had a wonderful flair for spotting a perfect location for establishing a monastery. None can ever have done better than the seventh century founders of Santo Toribio, which commands a superb panorama of some of the finest scenery of the Picos. The monastery buildings, in transitional Romanesque style, have recently been completely restored and are occupied by Franciscan monks.

The monastery has possessed since the eighth century what is claimed to be the largest fragment of the true Cross in existence, brought from Jerusalem by Saint Toribio himself. We arrived at the monastery chapel just as a young monk was taking the relic down from an altar for veneration by a large party of schoolchildren. I am afraid that I have made some derogatory remarks earlier about rioting parties of Spanish pupils. So it is only fair that I should record that in this instance their behaviour was impeccable. They filed past the reverend in an orderly manner, and each in turn reverently kissed the relic, which had been taken out of its magnificent gold and silver reliquary. We thought it appropriate to join the end of the queue.

This seemed to have pleased the young monk, because later he caught up with us and presented us with a pamphlet in several languages, including English, which set out in some detail the history of the relic through the centuries. The most interesting bit was at the end, where we read that the relic had recently been scientifically examined by forestry experts in Madrid, who had concluded that it was a fragment of a cypress tree some 2,000 years old. The pamphlet conceded that this in no way proved the authenticity of the relic, but that it at least kept open the possibility of it being a fragment of the genuine true Cross.

We read the pamphlet during an extended picnic on the grass in front of the monastery while admiring that incredible panorama. We were quite reluctant to bring to an end our foray into this remote and extraordinarily beautiful mountainous region. However, we were soon back on the coast road, where our last remaining objective was Santillana del Mar, described by Jean–Paul Sartre as the prettiest village in Spain. To reach it we passed through several more picturesque fishing villages, Unquera, St Vincente de Barquera (which seemed to consist almost entirely of fish restaurants), and Comillas, with a lovely old square rather spoiled by doubling as a car park.

Santillana del Mar is little more than two long streets both leading to a famous collegiate church. Those streets consist almost entirely of wonderfully preserved noblemen's residences of the fifteenth to the seventeenth centuries, most of which are decorated with highly ornamental and interesting coats of arms. The elegance of these fine old houses is enhanced by masses of flowers at every door and window and every other conceivable spot. The streets are still cobbled as in the pre-motorcar age, and no parking is permitted. The entire village has been declared a national monument.

It was permissible to drive, or rather bounce, through the cobbled streets to the collegiate church. The publicity material claims that the cloister is the most beautiful in Spain, a brave statement indeed, but probably not unjustified. The unusually short pillars bear intricately carved capitals which are claimed to be amongst the finest twelfth century sculpture to have survived. Since these capitals are at little more than head height, their remarkably beautiful designs can be admired and photographed to great advantage.

Santillana del Mar completed our planned itinerary. In many ways this had been the most memorable of all our journeys around Europe. It had also been much the longest and the most arduous, not helped by the fact that in the entrance to Leon Cathedral Rosemary had missed a step and damaged an ankle, and was in difficulties for the rest of the journey. We were now ready for the motorway to the French frontier, and then the shortest and quickest way home. As we sped along, however, there were some very strange names on the signposts, and we realised that we were now in the country of the Basques. One such name, 'Gernika-Luno' caught our attention, and we both immediately spotted the Spanish translation beneath, 'Guernica'.

It took us no time at all to decide that we must make one final short detour to visit this small town which figured so prominently, and tragically, in world news in 1937. Many of my pensioner readers will recall how news gradually filtered through that a calamity of new and unique proportions had occurred in that small Basque town. In the light of history we now know that Nazi bombers, in support of Franco's forces, killed over 2,000 innocent civilians, mostly on their way to their Saturday market. The massacre was later immortalised in the famous painting by Picasso.

However, when I visited the tourist information office, I could find no reference to 1937 or even Picasso. Instead the helpful young lady who welcomed this enquiring travel writer (I later did an article on Guernica for *Choice* magazine), wanted to talk only about Basque culture, history and nationalism, and the very flourishing modern town. The Basques, she explained, are very proud of being a people unique in Europe. Unlike other races who have come and gone, she said, the Basques have always been there in 'Euskadi'. Her claim would appear to be supported by their unique language, which seems to owe nothing at all to Greek, Latin, Hebrew or Arabic, and has a fiendishly complicated grammar.

The main historic sites are all close together on a hill in the centre of the town, and all mercifully escaped the German bombardment. First in importance is the 'Tree of Guernica', or rather two trees, the old and the new. For at least a thousand years the Basque parliament has gathered around this spot, generally to assert its independence from oppressors of one kind or another. The original oak tree, now a mere wizened stump, was transferred to a new site in 1983, when the devolved government for Euskadi was finally conceded and accepted. It now stands in rather incongruous splendour in a sort of cupola surrounded by Grecian pillars. A 'new' oak, planted last century, now flourishes in front of the 'Casa de Juntas', where general assemblies of the Basques have been held throughout the centuries.

The vast majority of Basques, said my informant in the tourist office, regard the settlement of 1983 as a satisfactory answer to their centuries-old nationalist aspirations. They are looking forward, she said, to a prosperous future under their devolved government. When I pressed her on the events of 1937, she presented that ghastly catastrophe as simply the last in the long catalogue of tragedies that the Basques have suffered in their long struggle for independence.

As we headed once again for the French frontier we reflected how the Basques seemed now to have very much the same acceptance of their new, devolved government as our friends in Catalonia, and the same positive attitude for the future. For the world at large, of course, Guernica 1937 was the prelude to Coventry, the London blitz, Dresden and finally, Hiroshima. We could only hope that the world has at last learned its lesson.

Safely back home, we reflected on our various adventures and experiences. We felt that it was somehow rather fitting that we should have ended our journey to Santiago de Compostela with that visit, albeit totally unpremeditated, to the place which, thanks to Picasso, is now the symbol of the Spanish War of the thirties. It was, after all, the involvement of Rosemary's cousin, Henry Buckley, in that war, and the subsequent generous hospitality of his family, and the encouragement of his son Raymond, that had stimulated our interest in travel in Spain in general, and the pilgrimage to Compostela in particular.

Interlude

I hope that it has been obvious from Part One of this book that my wife and I have enjoyed tremendously during our long retirement our independent exploration of Europe. We have always had an outline plan, of course, for each new expedition, but we have tried to be flexible and not let the plan take complete control. For instance, we have never hesitated to depart from the schedule and book in for the night at some inviting small hotel or 'chambre d'hôte' that has taken our fancy, such as the 'auberge rurale' near Fontaine de Vaucluse that I described in the chapter on Provence.

In small towns we have particularly enjoyed scrutinising for some possible local speciality the competing menus that are invariably displayed at the front of hotels and restaurants. We could even be flexible and opportunist with regard to the weather. When the skies were particularly favourable, we could linger longer in some idyllic rural spot; while on the occasional wet day we could treat the car as a sort of large mobile umbrella, and move on rapidly to our next destination.

We have particularly cherished our freedom to suspend the itinerary temporarily if something particularly interesting turns up unexpectedly. Let me give you an example. We were travelling north from Provence along the N88 heading for Le Puy, that unique city with all its major monuments perched precariously on pinnacles of rock, and happened to notice the name Le Monastier on a signpost pointing down a very minor road.

'Monastier', cried my knowledgeable wife, 'that's where Stevenson began his *Travels with a Donkey in the Cevennes*'. I knew that she was bound to be right; there was a shelf full of the works of R.L. Stevenson in a bookcase back home. So we made a *déviation* as the French call it, to see if the village was interesting.

We were surprised first of all to find ourselves crossing the River Loire, which was puzzling since we were half of France away from the chateaux of Chinon and Chenonceaux. Then we remembered that the Loire is the fourth longest river of Europe, and that this was evidently the infant Loire. We soon came to Le Monastier, which seemed to be largely one long straggling street. We knew we were getting warm when we passed a 'Bar Stevenson', and then a few yards further on came upon the 'Stevenson Memorial'. It was a quite modest plaque on a plinth that stated (in French):

> 'From here on the 22nd of September 1878 Robert
> Louis Stevenson set out on his journey through the
> Cevennes on a donkey.'

Our view of the inscription was partially obscured by three ladies sitting on a bench happily chatting and doing their knitting. Much to our embarrassment they insisted on rising in order to give us an uninterrupted view. They beamed with obvious pleasure; they were clearly delighted that these English visitors were showing the proper respect due to their village's literary renown.

These helpful ladies also informed us that there was another record of the famous journey in the Hotel de Ville. There we found one wall of the foyer of the town hall completely covered with a large illustrated plan of Stevenson's journey. We were pleased to note that attached to the map was a faded photograph of a donkey, which we took to be Modestine, though one donkey to the untutored eye looks very much like another. We felt that Modestine had deserved some recognition after the merciless manner in which Stevenson had apparently treated her, behaviour which might well have got him into trouble with the RSPCA in a later age.

The modern citizens of Monastier have clearly thought it prudent to forgive their celebrated visitor for his unflattering remarks about their ancestors, whom he describes as 'notable for drunkenness, freedom of language and unparalleled political dissension'. Over a hundred years later it appeared to be an entirely inoffensive, and indeed sleepy little town.

On another occasion — I hope that I am not prolonging this

interlude unbearably — we were driving briskly across Lorraine en route for Alsace which, with its enchanting 'villages enfleuris', is one of the most attractive provinces of France, and really deserved a chapter to itself in Part One of this book (except that Part One was in danger of becoming too long).

Lorraine, on the other hand, is largely industrial and uninviting, and we had no plans to linger there, until we suddenly discerned in the distance a huge cross of Lorraine some 150 feet high, and realised that we must have stumbled upon Colombey les Deux Églises, the home of General de Gaulle. 'Worth a visit', we thought to ourselves, in the words of the Michelin guide.

And so it proved, and later even worth an article in *The Observer*. The cross is on a hilltop just outside the village. You park your car and climb the hill on foot. The great cross stands in extensive formal gardens and is flanked by two engraved inscriptions from the more profound utterances of the General. The cross is huge and dignified, just as the General was in his lifetime. Apart from two rather bored-looking gendarmes who lurked unobtrusively in the background, we had the place to ourselves. Alongside is a museum of Gaullist memorabilia. Much the most interesting we thought was the original manuscript of the historic broadcast to the French people from London in 1940. There were so many scribbled corrections and crossings-out that it seemed largely illegible, rather like one of the notebooks of Beethoven.

In the village itself, de Gaulle's grave is simple in the extreme. The revered national hero could have been buried, I imagine, in appropriate splendour in Notre Dame, or with Napoléon in Les Invalides. However, he had expressed the wish to be buried beside his daughter Anne, who died in 1948 at the age of 20.

These were just two examples amongst many. This sort of opportunist rambling was ideal for France with all its many different provinces with their amazingly varied scenery, history, culture, customs and cuisine. Less so for Spain and Italy since the outline plan had to be followed more closely because of the long journey across France and a mountain range in between.

It was when we decided that we really must include Greece in our travels that the limitations of this unorganised form of holiday travel were borne in upon us. We studied the maps and were frankly intimidated. We live in the north of England. We would have to drive across England, France and Italy and undertake two ferry crossings before the visit even began. We decided that an organised tour was the only way to visit all the important classical sites in a holiday of reasonable length.

From the several possibilities on offer we selected a 'Saga' tour that from two centres covered the most important classical sites in two weeks. Thus began our love affair with Saga, that has lasted for nearly ten years and still continues.

PART TWO

Europe by
Saga Holidays

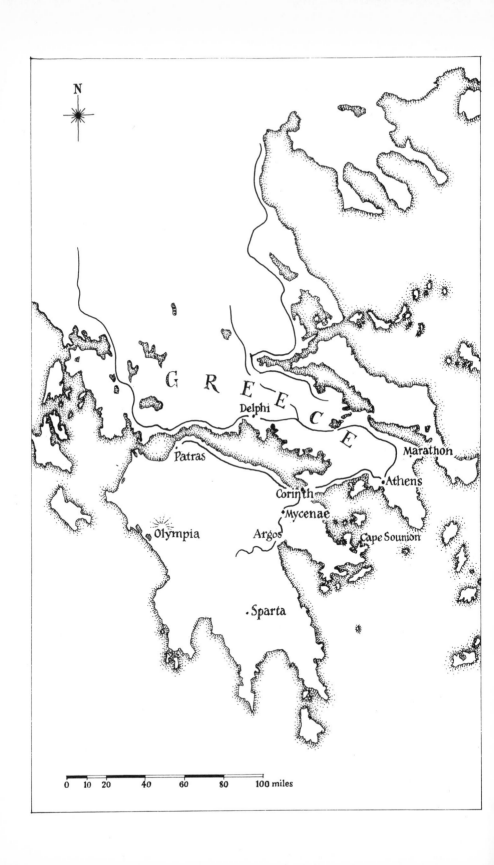

N

G R E E C E

Delphi

Patras

Marathon

Athens

Corinth

Olympia

Mycenae

Argos

Cape Sounion

Sparta

0 10 20   40   60   80   100 miles

CHAPTER SIX

Classical Greece

The charter plane whisked us from Gatwick to Glyfada airport near Athens in three and a half hours; we would have needed the best part of a week to get there by car and ferry. Our first impressions of Saga were encouraging; we were met by helpful representatives at Euston, Victoria, Gatwick and Glyfada, and our luggage was taken care of at each stage of the journey.

Once we were standing on the Acropolis at Athens any misgivings about the wisdom of our mode of travel rapidly evaporated. Despite the great crowds of every nation struggling up the steep and slippery slope of the Propylaea, the ancient gateway to the Acropolis, and the minor distraction of the inevitable restoration work in progress, the impact of those gleaming white columns of the Parthenon, quite dazzling in the midday sun, was simply overwhelming.

As a one-time student and teacher of the classics, I naturally found the experience of at last gazing on these famous monuments quite moving. I remembered how I used to maintain in my lectures to my sixth-form students that, apart from our Christian religion, everything of real value in our modern world, art, literature, philosophy, even our very system of democratic government, stemmed from that remarkable Greek civilisation which originated here in Athens, and which the Romans later spread over most of western Europe.

The distinguished scholar, Professor H.D.F. Kitto, in his book *The Greeks*, wrote that 'The contribution made to Greek and European culture by this one city is quite astonishing, and, unless our standards of civilisation are comfort and contraptions, Athens in the fifth and fourth centuries BC was clearly the most civilised society that ever existed'.

The Parthenon, the Erechtheum, the Temple of Nike and the rest of the buildings on the Acropolis were even more impressive at night, when we were taken to a 'son et lumière' presentation. It was again quite exciting to take our seats on the hill of the Pnyx where such as Pericles and Demosthenes used to harangue their fellow citizens when they met to debate and decide the important issues of peace and war. Each of the famous monuments of the Acropolis was picked out for us in turn, and highlighted in the brilliance of the floodlights. The 'lumière' part of this presentation was, however, distinctly superior to the 'son'. The script, based on the history of the Persian Wars, was at times positively corny, and the inevitable background music irritatingly inappropriate. Nevertheless, it was for me an experience never to be forgotten, and certainly worth every penny, or rather every drachma, of the entrance fee.

After the Acropolis at Athens, our greatest thrill was at Mycenae. There we passed first through the legendary Lion Gate, which was built around 1250 BC and unbelievably still survives in recognisable shape. We then gazed down into the great hole, where in 1876 the German archaeologist Schliemann revealed the amazingly sophisticated civilisation that flourished over a thousand years before the time of those that we think of as the 'Ancient Greeks'. Schliemann has had a rather rough time at the hands of some later scholars, because his excavation techniques were relatively crude compared with more modern methods, and because he got his dates wrong by a mere 500 years or so. That was when in his understandable excitement he sent off his flamboyant telegram saying, 'I have gazed upon the face of Agamemnon'.

However, the man's achievement was undeniably colossal, as was certainly brought home to us in the Mycenaean room of the National Archaeological Museum in Athens. There we, too, gazed upon the marvellous golden death mask that Schliemann mistakenly attributed to Agamemnon, and the thousands of other astonishing exhibits from those tombs that illustrate the incredible sophistication of that almost prehistoric civilisation.

A dedicated classical scholar could profitably spend several days in that museum in Athens, which probably houses the finest collection of Greek art in the world. It was interesting to note that the

collection has been significantly added to in recent years by finds of bronze statues in the seas around the coasts of the Mediterranean. These include a bronze thought to be by the great sculptor Praxitiles hauled out of the sea off Marathon in 1925. The most notable example of this salvage of ancient treasures from the sea was the Bronzes of Riace which I mention in the later chapter on Sicily and southern Italy. These, now in the National Museum at Reggio di Calabria, were discovered only 20 years ago, after lying there for well over 2,000 years. It makes one wonder what further finds may still come to light.

Back in Athens we naturally made more visits to the area round the Acropolis while we had the chance, as well as to the other places that were essential parts of that remarkable Athenian system of democratic government. The nearby rocky hill of the Areopagus was the site of the Supreme Court of Athens. Presumably the ascent of the hill must have been easier in ancient times than it is now, when it involves almost a minor rock climb. One simply could not imagine those venerable judges tackling that ascent on a daily basis. Nevertheless the effort is certainly worth while for the reasonably agile tourist, since from the top of the Areopagus there is a tremendous view over the Agora which was the heart of the city and the general meeting place for business transactions, and where the likes of Socrates, Plato and Aristotle used to stroll and hold their profound philosophical discussions.

It was also on the Areopagus that we first remembered that this area of Greece was equally important in the history of the early Christian Church, and that St Paul made some of his first converts here. A modern bronze tablet fixed to the rock face commemorates this fact, and quotes from the Acts of the Apostles, Chapter 17, part of his famous sermon to the Council of the Areopagus. 'I noticed,' he said, 'as I strolled around admiring your sacred monuments, that you had an altar inscribed "To An Unknown God". Well, the God whom I proclaim is in fact the one you already worship without knowing it.'

Our interest in St Paul's activities in these parts having been thus aroused, we made a visit to the spot where, according to tradition, he first set foot in Greece. This by coincidence is less than a mile from Glyfada International Airport where we, like thousands of other tourists, also first arrived in Greece. The apostle disembarked here in the year AD 50, presumably from a more primitive form of transport. The Greeks in general tend their historic places with loving care. This unfortunately is an exception. The supposed precise spot of St Paul's arrival is marked by the ruins of a seventh century church. The scanty remains are choked with weeds and enclosed by a rusty, broken down, barbed-wire fence.

We caught up with St Paul again on our visit to the ancient city of Corinth. Not quite so ancient as all that, however. We had forgotten that Corinth was ruthlessly razed to the ground by the Roman Lucius Mummius in 146 BC, but rebuilt a century later at the insistence of Julius Caesar, no less. It was therefore in this relatively 'modern' city of Corinth that the apostle worked and preached. One can still see the 'bema' or rostrum at which he was arraigned before the Roman Pro-Consul (Acts XVIII, 12-18).

Another awe-inspiring visit was to the oracle of Delphi, pre-eminently the most holy site in the world of ancient Greece. The oracle in the temple of Apollo on the slopes of Mount Parnassus was constantly consulted on political and even domestic matters by pilgrims from all over the Greek world and beyond. And despite the 'oracular' or ambiguous nature of the priestesses' replies, it retained its unique status for many centuries. Some of the oracle's more famous pronouncements have survived. Perhaps the best known concerns the legendary King Croesus of Lydia. He was told by the oracle that if he invaded the kingdom of Cyrus the Great, King of Persia, he would destroy a mighty empire. Greatly encouraged he went ahead, but the empire that he destroyed was his own.

The modern village of Delphi dates only from AD 1892 when the inhabitants were transferred to a new site to permit French archaeologists to excavate the temple of Apollo. Somewhere in between the two is a fine purpose-built museum that contains the best of the discoveries from the excavations. Much the most celebrated of these is the Bronze Charioteer of Delphi, one of the finest works of art to have survived from the fifth century BC.

We visited another fine museum at Olympia, quite one of the most spacious and generally impressive that we have seen. Here, rightly accorded the privilege of a room to himself, is perhaps the most notable marble statue to have come down to us relatively intact from the greatest period of Greek sculpture, the Hermes of Praxitiles. The sight of the Hermes was a rather special experience for me, since I remembered answering a question on Praxitiles in my degree exam. I didn't expect then to have to wait half a century before actually seeing his masterpiece in the flesh — or rather the marble!

The Olympic stadium itself at first seemed disappointingly small, indeed almost insignificant compared to the vast venues of the modern Olympic Games. Until one remembered that in the very beginning there was only a single race, the foot-race round the stadium, although more events were introduced later. The modest length of the stadium, 183 metres, was supposed to have been decreed by the legendary hero Herakles.

There once stood on this temple site one of the so-called Seven Wonders of the Ancient World, the gigantic statue of Zeus by Pheidias, constructed of gold and ivory. The statue was transported to Constantinople by the Roman Emperor Theodosius and finally perished in a fire. Fragments of the blue stone that formed the base of the statue are still visible at Olympia, as are the remains of the artist's workshop. Nearby is the altar at which the flame is kindled at the start of the modern Olympic Games and then conveyed by relays of runners to Rome, Barcelona or wherever.

The traditional date of the first Olympiad was 776 BC, and the festivals continued uninterruptedly at four-year intervals for over a thousand years, till AD 393. There have been some strange goings-on and some colourful competitors in recent Olympic Games, but none can quite have compared with the games of AD 67, when the star competitor was the Emperor Nero. Despite twice falling off his horse, he was still the winner in the chariot race, and he also won the singing contest which had been specially introduced for his benefit. He finally departed for Rome with some 500 priceless ancient statues as his prize.

As a break from the round of classical antiquities, we opted for a one-day cruise which allowed a few hours on each of three islands, Aegina, Poros and Hydra. All three looked unbelievably beautiful as we approached them across the brilliant blue of the Aegean, but especially Hydra, which is one of the few remaining inhabited places on earth where no cars disturb the peace. Transport on Hydra is restricted to mule, donkey or boat.

Back on the mainland we drove to Marathon, scene of the great decisive battle against the Persian invaders in 490 BC, and finally to Cape Sounion where the remains of the Temple of Poseidon stand on the southernmost point of Attica. Here our local guide proudly pointed out possibly the most celebrated of all graffiti, the signature of Lord Byron engraved on one of those precious pillars. If you or I had done it, we would have been damned as mindless vandals and hooligans, but for a great poet and dedicated philhellene, it's apparently all right.

Our visits to Delphi and Olympia were made from a second base near Patras in the Pelopennese. The city of Patras itself is mainly notable for its imposing modern Greek Orthodox Church of St Andrew. Here in a magnificent reliquary is housed the skull of the apostle and substantial portions of the X-shaped cross on which, according to tradition, he was martyred on this very spot. These precious relics, after centuries in the Vatican in Rome, were restored to the Greek Orthodox Church by Pope Paul VI in 1965 as a gesture of ecumenical goodwill.

From Patras we also made an excursion through superb mountain scenery to the village of Kalavytra and two nearby monasteries. Kalavytra is a rather depressing little place, remembered as the scene of one of the worst Nazi atrocities in the Second World War. The church clock remains permanently fixed at 2.34 pm, the precise hour at which all the males of the village were massacred in a savage act of revenge.

Like so many monasteries in Europe, those of Agia Lavra and Mega Spelion were perched high up on seemingly inaccessible sites. We averted our gaze as the driver nonchalantly hauled our coach round the hairpin bends with his off-side wheels perilously close to the chasm below. At Mega Spelion there is a relic of another of the early fathers of the church, the evangelist St Luke. A monk reverently revealed in a protective safe in a wall the monastery's treasured possession, the ikon of the Blessed Virgin, which St Luke himself is supposed to have painted.

And so our Saga Tour of Classical Greece gave us more for our money than we had expected. There was another welcome bonus as well, the agreeable company of like-minded veterans both on tour and especially at dinner in the evenings, men and women with a lifetime of accumulated experience and a wealth of wit and wisdom in conversation. I will just quote one after-dinner conversation over the coffee in the lounge that I remember well.

Our visits to the Parthenon and also to those magnificent museums at Delphi and Olympia sparked off a discussion one evening on the current controversy with regard to the continuing retention in the British Museum of the Elgin Marbles, whose return, of course, has been repeatedly demanded by the Greek government. There was complete agreement that Lord Elgin, whatever his motives may have been, had contrived just in the nick of time to preserve for posterity those supreme masterpieces of Greek sculpture. On the morality of the continued retention by our country of what are obviously an important part of the national heritage of Greece, there were conflicting opinions.

The wretched condition of the sculptures remaining *in situ* on the Parthenon, plus the Athenians' apparently insuperable problems with air pollution, clearly ruled out their restoration to their original position. However, there was probably a majority opinion that if the Greek government was prepared to house the marbles in a similar purpose-built museum to those at Delphi and Olympia, there was a strong moral imperative to restore our ill-gotten goods.

There was also unanimous agreement that our Saga package tour had introduced us most satisfactorily to the 'Glory That Was Greece'. We were less certain about the glories of contemporary Greece. It is difficult, for instance, to enthuse about the modern city of Athens. It seems to have exploded into a capital of over three million inhabitants far too quickly and with far too little planning. It has few of the elegant boulevards of Paris, the majestic vistas of London, or the gracious old buildings of Vienna or Amsterdam, and the process seems to be continuing. In the outskirts of Athens one could see hibiscus and tamarisk and shady palms and giant cacti in abundance, but all fighting for survival in a chaotic rash of new building sites.

However, there were two pleasant features of the modern city that in all fairness I ought to mention. First the all-pervading Greek folk music with lilting melodies on balalaikas and bazookas, so much more soothing and musical than the equivalent British pop. Secondly the bus fares, one modest charge for any distance in this great sprawling city. Our fellow travellers from Dundee to Devon, and especially London, were incredulously comparing their fares back home.

The Bronze Charioteer of Delphi, Greece

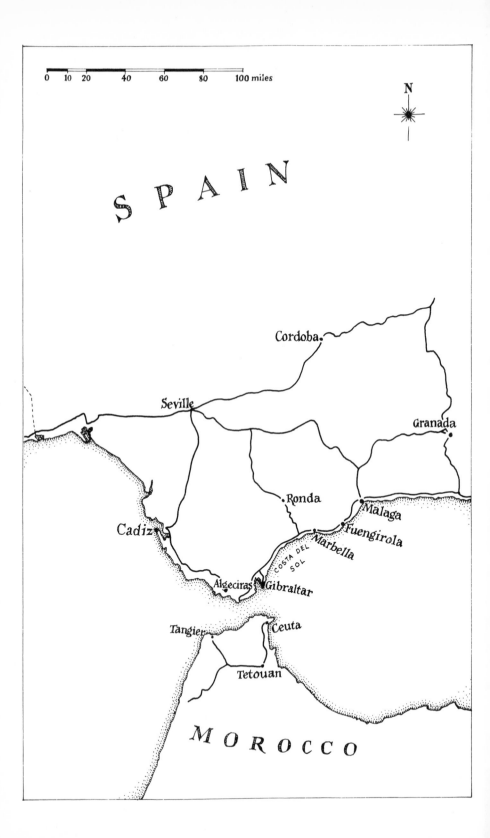

N

0 10 20   40   60   80   100 miles

S P A I N

Cordoba.

Seville

Granada

.Ronda

Malaga

Cadiz

Fuengirola
Marbella
COSTA DEL
SOL

Algeciras Gibraltar

Tangier Ceuta

Tetouan

M O R O C C O

CHAPTER SEVEN

Spain–Andalucia

W e had crossed our Rubicon; we had enjoyed our first package tour and at the same time experienced at last 'The Glory That Was Greece'. The experience had been far less fraught and far more rewarding than we could ever have imagined.

We naturally asked ourselves next whether there were other more distant parts of western Europe that we were anxious to visit, and for which a Saga tour might also be the right answer. We immediately thought of Andalucia in southern Spain, with those legendary cities Seville, Cordoba and Granada, where a Moorish civilisation of great sophistication flourished for some 700 years.

Andalucia had not figured previously in our plans for travel in Spain for two good reasons. The first obviously was the distance. A journey by car, involving virtually the whole of England, France and Spain, and back again, would leave precious little time for exploring Andalucia itself in a holiday of reasonable length. The second reason was that for our journeys around Spain we had obviously taken advantage first of the kindness of Rosemary's Spanish (or, as they would prefer) Catalan cousins, who had generously pressed hospitality upon us in Catalonia, Castile and the mountains above Madrid, but who had no houses to lend in Andalucia. Nevertheless, our professor cousin Raymond, whom I spoke of at length in the chapter on Catalonia in Part One, and who had masterminded our pilgrimage to Compostela, also described in Part One, was insistent that our next visit to Spain should be to the cities of Andalucia. Another Saga tour was the obvious answer.

As I mentioned in the previous chapter, one of the most pleasant discoveries of our first Saga holiday had been the congenial company, and the ease with which we made new friends. It occurred to us that we could go one better this time; we could take our friends with us. We knew that two of our wartime friends, with whom we had always kept in close touch, were also inveterate travellers in Europe. Jack and Rina, after hearing of our happy experiences in Greece, accepted with alacrity our invitation to join us.

If we had any misgivings about the itinerary outlined in the brochure for the Andalucian holiday, it was that the tour began and ended on the notorious Costa del Sol. We were to begin indeed with two full days at Fuengirola, one of the most popular resorts, and we viewed the prospect with mild dismay as rather a waste of valuable time. We needn't have worried; two exciting one-day excursions were available from Fuengirola, the first to the city of Ronda and the second across the Mediterranean to Tetouan in Morocco.

We particularly looked forward to visiting Ronda. Our afore-mentioned cousin Raymond annually conducted his American students round the sights of Andalucia, and with great emphasis he urged us on no account to omit Ronda from our trip. 'Don't miss Ronda,' he said, 'even if it should mean leaving out Cordoba or Seville.' Fortunately it only required us to omit, with no reluctance at all, a day on the Costa del Sol.

So we had a mounting sense of anticipation as our coach left behind the endless succession of identical hotels and dreary shape-less blocks of apartments that have submerged under a sea of con-crete the once beautiful coastline of Andalucia from Malaga to Algeciras. Shortly after passing Marbella and the private mosque of the king of Saudi Arabia, a rare point of interest on this generally featureless road, we turned north and begun the long tortuous climb to the mountains.

After some 30 miles through the brown and parched coun-tryside with which we were already familiar in central parts of Spain, we reached the point nearly 2,500 feet above sea level where the city of Ronda stands on its quite incredible site above the valley of the River Guadalevin more than 300 feet below. The citizens of Ronda are understandably proud of their city's unique situation. The official guide book waxes lyrical and speaks of 'this seemingly inaccessible town, next to the clouds and the stars, overlooking the terrible gorge at its feet', and later in the same passage 'Like an eagle's nest it lies peacefully suspended between the stars and the abyss'.

Ronda has been in the itinerary of travellers and writers ever since Pliny and Strabo in the first century AD, who knew it as 'Arunda', the city surrounded by mountains. Richard Ford, in his *Hand-book for Travellers in Spain* in 1845, wrote 'There is only one Ronda in the world . . . The scene, its noise and movement, baffle pen and pencil; we can only exclaim, "Well done, rock and water, by heavens"!'

An American standing alongside us put the same thing more pungently if less poetically. 'Gee,' he exclaimed, 'why the heck should any guy want to build a city here?' He might well wonder. As one gazes down from the Puente Nuevo, the great bridge built across the gorge in 1788 to join two communities previously separated by 'El Tajo', the yawning chasm, one does indeed wonder what on earth could motivate successive generations and many different races to want to inhabit this inhospitable and almost inaccessible spot.

Yet scholars have established that prehistoric man was here from the cave paintings that he left behind. Celts, Phoenicians, Carthaginians, and of course, the Romans, all followed. Finally the Arabs, during their long occupation of most of Spain, developed Ronda into one of their strongest fortresses in Andalucia. Inevitably, therefore, Ferdinand and Isabella, the Catholic monarchs, found Ronda the toughest and fiercest point of Arab resistance after 700 years of occupation. When, after months of campaigning, Ronda the impregnable finally fell to the Christian troops, Ferdinand returned in triumph to Cordoba to receive a rapturous welcome from Isabella.

Despite its remote and isolated situation, Ronda has surprisingly made some notable contributions to the Spanish way of life. Andalucia is almost synonymous with the art of flamenco. Vincente Espinel, a citizen of Ronda, has an important place in the history of art as the man who introduced the distinctive fifth string to the flamenco guitar. However, the inhabitants' greatest pride is unquestionably in their bullring, which they claim to be the oldest in Spain and the cradle of the art of classical bullfighting technique. It was at

Ronda, we were told, that Francisco Romero founded the modern school of bullfighters. His descendants carried on the tradition, and among these his grandson Pedro Romero, in a long and highly acclaimed career, had the dubious distinction of killing 5,530 bulls, no less. He died peacefully in his bed at the age of 85!

Before taking us to visit this historic shrine of bullfighting, our guide subjected us to a little lecture. He begged us to forget our British prejudices and to realise that the matador requires not only nerves of steel, but also grace and skill equal to that of a great ballet dancer. Bullfighting, he assured us, is the supreme Spanish art form, a most important part of Spanish culture and the Spanish way of life.

After this little homily, spoken with great passion and conviction, it came as something of an anti-climax to discover that this famous home of bullfighting now stages only one event a year. Our guide rather lamely and sorrowfully explained that since the ring was small and housed only 5,000 spectators, it could no longer compete with the vast stadiums of the big cities. Apparently, like the once famous British small-town football clubs now languishing in the lower divisions of the Football League, such as Huddersfield Town, Burnley, and, nearest to my heart, Preston North End, Ronda bullfighting has fallen victim to the inexorable pressures of economics and market forces.

We found lots of other more pleasant places of interest in Ronda, an Arab minaret, Arab baths and several notable churches, especially the Church of Santa Maria de la Mayor. This, originally a Moorish mosque, was enlarged and converted into a Christian church on the express orders of Ferdinand and Isabella. We particularly admired its immensely ornate interior.

There are also a number of Renaissance-style palaces in the town. We visited one of these, the Casa de Mondragon, a beautifully furnished and elegant old building which has been adapted as a home for old priests. It was nice to see these retired reverends relaxing in the sunshine in the delightful gardens, from where they could enjoy those stunning views over the gorge to the valley beyond.

It is, of course, this spectacular setting which is nine-tenths of the tourist appeal of the city of Ronda. We couldn't quite agree with cousin Raymond that Ronda is the number one attraction in Andalucia, outstripping in interest even Seville or Cordoba. However, we were certainly glad to have had the opportunity to stand on the Puente Nuevo and experience that unique view over El Tajo — the view which one writer in a desperate search for an adequate adjective has described as 'paralysing'. We, too, felt lost for words.

After this thoroughly exciting and quite memorable excursion to the city of Ronda, we had another spare day in Fuengirola before moving on to Seville to begin the real business of the holiday. A short stroll through Fuengirola on the day of arrival had done nothing to lessen our prejudices about the Spanish Costas. We happen to live less than 20 miles from the Golden Mile at Blackpool, and we found the promenade at Fuengirola frighteningly reminiscent, except that the weather was distinctly better. There were the same English-style fast food stalls and cheapjack souvenir shops. One food shop was even offering 'Auntie Maggie's apple pie'!

So we were delighted to discover that we could be liberated from languishing a whole day on the Costa by taking another optional excursion, this time across the Mediterranean to Tetouan in North Africa. Jack and Rina understandably decided that two excursions in two days were too exacting and expensive, and decided instead to relax in the elegant gardens of our hotel. Rosemary and I had never been to Africa, however, and felt that this was too good an opportunity to miss. As for the expense, I arrogantly announced that I was sure I could recoup that by writing one of my travel articles about the trip, and I actually did so a few months later. Rosemary brightly suggested a title for the piece, 'One Toe Into Africa', but an unimaginative editor preferred 'Day Trip to Morocco'.

We sailed from Algeciras and soon had a fine close-up view of the Rock of Gibraltar. All the many Spaniards of our acquaintance, even ardent Anglophiles, regard Gibraltar as self-evidently a part of Spain, and its continuing occupation by the British as simply one of those irritating eccentricities for which the British are notorious. Our Spanish guide was gently sarcastic. He was at pains to point out that from the boat we were able to see two continents, Europe and Africa, and no less than three countries, Spain, Morocco and — Great Britain! We were therefore all the more surprised to discover on our arrival on the coast of Africa that we were still in Spain. The Spaniards, in fact, have their own Gibraltar, as it were, in the free port of Ceuta, which they insisted on retaining when the rest of Morocco gained its independence in 1956.

There were tedious delays at the Moroccan frontier. Some members of our party were considerably upset by the requirement of the frontier police that we surrender our passports till our return later in the day. Some Americans in the Saga party, who generally added notably to the gaiety of the holiday, were particularly indignant. 'I've always been taught never to let my US passport out of my sight,' shouted one rebellious Yank. It was only when our local guide quietly explained that unless he was willing to comply, the whole visit was off for everybody, that with great reluctance he finally handed it over.

Our coach departed at last into Morocco. The drive at first was disappointing, along a Moroccan coastline that was featureless and desolate, but things brightened up when we stopped in a spacious lay-by and were invited to try our skill at riding camels. We politely declined, but some enterprising veterans in our party, particularly from among the group of Americans, displayed surprising agility and fortitude in mounting and hanging on to these awkward beasts, amidst great hilarity and much photography.

We arrived at the centre of the city of Tetouan nicely in time for lunch. This turned out to be interesting and substantial. A fairly unremarkable soup was followed by couscous. We had met this rather exotic dish before in the south of France, but here presumably was the authentic recipe — chicken cooked with granulated flour and saffron. This was followed by a huge slice of melon and mint tea.

Feeling reasonably fortified, we went off for our visit to the bazaars. First, however, we were given dire warnings by our guide to keep closely together, to watch our purses and handbags incessantly, and under no circumstances to photograph military establishments or even soldiers or policemen, unless we wanted to end up in a Moroccan jail.

It was like entering another world. We found ourselves in a warren of narrow, winding alleys indescribable in their chaos and confusion. It was almost impossible to keep closely in touch with our guide, as instructed, since he was soon lost in the noisy crowds milling around the long line of stalls piled high with miscellaneous produce. There was an almost equal quantity of vegetables and other foods simply standing in heaps on the ground.

Remembering the stringent rules of food hygiene with which we are familiar at home, it was slightly nauseating to see meat and fish stalls simply crawling with flies. We tried not to wonder from which stall the meat for our lunch-time couscous had been purchased. Occasionally a boy with a fly swatter would lazily move the flies on from one piece of meat to the next. There were a disturbing number of ailing and crippled old people in evidence, while beggars were operating everywhere. Even quite healthy-looking young children were brazenly pestering us for money at every turn.

A snake charmer provided a welcome diversion. We were persuaded by our guide to gather, somewhat hesitantly, close around his pitch. He first released from his bag several nasty-looking cobras, which obediently uncoiled themselves and swayed menacingly to and fro. We were considerably disappointed that the snake charmer didn't play suitably exotic music on a pipe. Evidently these were a kind of snake that didn't need music while they worked!

As his *tour de force*, the snake charmer produced a swathe of further slimy creatures which he draped around his neck. He then invited a volunteer from among the onlookers to be similarly adorned. Sure enough, George, the likeable, elderly Yank who had been first up on a camel, submitted with a suitably deadpan expression to allow the snakes, presumably some harmless variety, to be festooned around his neck. More hilarity, of course, and more pictures to show to the folks back home.

On our way back to our coach we were simply bombarded by a horde of super-salesmen, youths offering leather goods, mainly handbags, at prices which, as we resisted, they steadily reduced. As we retreated from the onslaught into the coach, they became positively frantic, beating on the windows of the coach with their handbags, and screaming offers of ever better bargains.

On the return journey our passports were duly restored without any fuss at all at the border with Ceuta, and the Americans, in particular, were mightily relieved. As we sailed back across the Straits, we certainly had plenty to think about. Even more so the next day, when we visited at last the glories of the civilisation left behind by the Moors in Seville. It was hard indeed to realise that the inspiration for so much beauty had come from the same north Africa where we had just been witnesses of so much depressing poverty and squalor. Our 'One Toe Into Africa' had certainly been an eye-opener — to mix a few metaphors.

Seville, rather like Venice and Vienna, is a city whose name immediately evokes a mixture of pleasurable associations. The Barber, bitter oranges, Don Juan, flamenco; Seville can suggest any or all of these. Almost all the guide books quote an old proverb 'Quien no ha visto Sevilla no ha visito maravilla' — 'Who has not seen Seville has not seen a marvel'. Indeed, there are many contrasting marvels. On the one hand Seville is a wonderfully handsome city, its great parks and broad leafy avenues almost reminiscent of Paris. On the other hand there are enchanting narrow, winding, whitewashed streets with tiny patios smothered in flowers, notably in the Barrio de Santa Cruz, the one-time Jewish ghetto.

As he gathered us together on our arrival in Seville, however, our guide spoke first of none of these marvels, but rather of muggers and bag snatchers. He was an engaging little fellow and clearly a dedicated patriot. 'It pains me to speak in this way of my country,' he said with great earnestness, 'but Seville is a dangerous city'. We took due note of his warning, but as we emerged into the brilliant sunshine of a warm October day, such unpleasant thoughts were soon forgotten.

We found Seville's spacious and elegant parks immensely attractive, and especially the Parque Maria Luisa. This great expanse was redesigned in 1929 to house a celebrated Ibero-American exhibition. Several of the national pavilions from this exhibition are still in use, most notably the Spanish pavilion itself, which is now the headquarters of the Spanish army and sweeps in a great semi-circle

round the vast Plaza de España, and is encircled by a narrow canal with four picturesque bridges. A particularly delightful feature of the Parque Maria Luisa is a resident flock of perfectly white doves, not the notorious common or garden pigeons found in less favoured cities such as Venice. From time to time these beautiful birds suddenly sweep up into the sky in the brilliant sunlight with dazzling effect. Almost as impressive are the Murillo gardens, named after the famous artist, who was one of Seville's favourite sons. Both sets of gardens, with their towering palm trees, giant cacti and various exotic shrubs, provide a welcome oasis of shade in the all-pervading heat.

Across the road from the Parque Maria Luisa is a huge rather forbidding-looking building which originally was a tobacco factory, but is now a part of the University of Seville. We were surprised to learn that it had become redundant in its earlier role, because we had noticed that so many of the beautiful dark-haired senoritas that we passed in the street were smoking cigarettes. One of our Spanish friends explained to us later that after the end of the Franco regime, smoking unfortunately became something of a symbol of female emancipation in Spain.

The cathedral of Seville is unquestionably one of the most remarkable in Europe. In the first place a Moorish mosque was demolished to make way for it. There was then erected what is claimed to be the largest Gothic building in the world and the third largest cathedral after St Peter's in Rome and St Paul's in London. Finally it houses the tomb of Christopher Columbus. This most unusual and striking monument dominates the south transept of the cathedral and consists of a coffin borne aloft on the shoulders of the kings of Navarre, Aragon, Leon and Castile. It was originally erected in Havana, but was moved to Spain when Cuba gained her independence in 1898.

I don't know what the Spanish is for *embarras de richesse*, but whatever it is, Seville Cathedral has it. The place is an absolute treasure house of art of all kinds of many nations — gorgeous golden altar-pieces in the many side chapels, masses of priceless silverware in the sacristy, masterpieces by Murillo, Goya, Zurbaran and Ribera on the walls, wrought-iron grilles, stained glass windows and marble and tiled floors.

Some of the finest of these treasures can be admired in the Capilla Real, the Royal Chapel. Under an immense dome, decorated with the heads of kings, stands a beautiful, robed statue of La Virgen de los Reyes, Our Lady of the Monarchs, and patroness of Seville. This ancient statue is said to date from the thirteenth century, and to have been presented to King Ferdinand, the liberator of Seville, by his cousin St Louis, King of France. Ferdinand himself, also a saint, lies buried in a superb silver casket immediately below the statue.

Inscribed in large letters over the altar in this Capilla Real are the words 'Per Me Reges Regnant', one of those succinct Latin sentences so difficult to translate adequately into English. Perhaps one might suggest 'Kings rule with God's permission'. It is a thought that might usefully be placed on the desks of our modern rulers, presidents and prime ministers.

We had just one small reservation about the cathedral of Seville. As in many other Spanish cathedrals that we have visited, notably Segovia and Saragossa, one's view of the many fine altars and their wonderful works of art is sadly restricted by the need to peer through the heavy wrought-iron screens of which the Spaniards are so inordinately fond, even though these screens are, of course, themselves usually superb examples of Spanish craftsmanship.

The cathedral of Seville possesses one further 'marvel' that is this time unquestionably unique. Attached to the cathedral building is the Giralda tower, which is a Moorish minaret, a splendid example of Arab art, and the unrivalled symbol of the city of Seville, which therefore inevitably appears in every picture of the city. One guide book, in fact, incongruously names it the 'Eiffel Tower' of Seville. It was built around 1190 by the Moorish caliph Abu Yacub Yusuf.

After the recapture of Seville from the Arabs and the demolition of the Moorish mosque to make way for the massive cathedral, there was apparently a public outcry at the prospect of a similar fate befalling the beloved minaret. (It must have been similar to the outrage generated nowadays when official vandals propose to run a motorway extension through some popular beauty spot such as

Twyford Down.) So the Moorish minaret was reprieved and incorporated into the Christian cathedral as its bell-tower.

An ascent of Giralda is more or less obligatory for all visitors to Seville, but there is a problem; the tower is over 300 feet high and there is no lift! There is a beguiling notice at the entrance to the tower which says 'Easy walk'. Actually the ascent, most unusually, is by a wide, gently sloping ramp which winds round the tower about 30 times before the breathless climber emerges to enjoy a superb panorama over the roof-tops of Seville and the loop of the great River Guadalquivir. Apparently this highly unusual arrangement was originally designed to enable gentlemen on horseback to make the ascent without dismounting. We were rather pleased that we met no horses on our way up or down.

Seville's other great tourist attraction is its Moorish Alcazar, conveniently close to the cathedral, but partially concealed by great rough walls which give it at first sight the misleading aspect of a medieval fortress. Within, however, there is revealed a masterpiece of that mudejar style of architecture which flowered in the early Christian era, heavily influenced by Moorish traditions. Our guide led us through a series of magnificent rooms, all exquisitely decorated with marvellously intricate variations on the severely abstract designs that the Moslem religion required. We noted as well many particularly fine examples of the 'azulejos' or ceramic wall tiles, which are always an outstanding feature of these mudejar buildings.

Attached to the Alcazar, again enclosed within high walls spectacularly smothered in colourful bougainvillaea, is yet another of those exotic gardens which are such a welcome refuge from the all-pervading heat of Andalucia. Here the Alcazar gardens with orange groves, huge palm trees, fountains, fishponds and meticulously trimmed hedges provided an oasis of shade on terraces and patios.

I doubt whether in all our travels around Europe we have ever experienced a more breathtaking moment than our first sight of the interior of the Mezquita, the great mosque of Cordoba. We gazed almost with disbelief on a seemingly endless forest of pillars, 850 in all, in pink and blue marble and alabaster, supporting hundreds of two-tiered arches in red and white stripes. The magnitude and magnificence of the Mezquita, as it is still known, reflects the fact that Cordoba was the heart and capital of Islamic Spain, and at its zenith in the ninth century the foremost city of Europe. The mosque was begun in 785, was enlarged later several times, and at first survived intact the capture of Cordoba by Saint King Ferdinand in 1236. It was simply reconsecrated as a Christian church and dedicated to the Virgin of the Assumption.

However, some 300 years later, after the 'reconquista', the final recapture of the whole of Spain from the Moors by the 'Catholic monarchs' Ferdinand and Isabella, the Christian authorities of Cordoba were not satisfied with the makeshift arrangement of their converted mosque. So, despite bitter and furious protests, as at Seville in the case of the Giralda tower, they settled for the extraordinary compromise of demolishing some 60 columns and erecting a Gothic cathedral in the middle of the mosque. There is an often quoted story of Charles V, the Holy Roman Emperor and grandson of Ferdinand and Isabella. Although he had originally given his approval to the plans, he later regarded the work in progress with distinctly modified rapture. 'You have destroyed something unique,' he is reported to have remarked, 'to build something commonplace'.

On this first visit to the Mezquita we saw a notice indicating that there was Mass in the cathedral each weekday morning at 9.30. So we decided to go along. I should explain, perhaps, that as Catholics ourselves, we have rather made a point in our travels around Europe of attending Mass, wherever possible, in each country that we visit. We counted up once that we have heard Mass in 14 different languages. (On one occasion, in a country district of Alsace, we had the sermon twice, once in French and then again in a wholly incomprehensible Alsatian dialect of German.) As one would expect in the universal church, the essentials of the Mass are always recognisably the same, but it is fascinating to see the widely differing regional variations in the procedures, which often reflect local interests, artistic and musical.

Never before, anywhere in Europe, however, had we found ourselves at half past nine on an ordinary weekday morning attending a Mass in a cathedral within a mosque. And it was no ordinary Mass, but rather a sung High Mass, complete with incense and organ, concelebrated by at least a dozen priests with as many more in support. All these clergy were sporting that curious ecclesiastical headgear called a biretta, unknown in our part of the world for many a year. Some of them even had green pom-poms on their birettas, which we took to be a mark of seniority.

We were particularly fascinated by the organist, who never permitted a moment's silence, and, whenever the choir were not singing, contributed *fortissimo* wholly inappropriate and unliturgical selections from Bach and Beethoven. One of the Americans in our Saga party who had joined us, whispered in my ear, 'Gee, that organist guy is sure having a ball!' The Mass ended at 10.30, the official opening time for the mosque, when the tourists flooded in, including our friends Jack and Rina. We were amused that they had to pay an entrance fee of about a pound apiece, while we, as an extra bonus for getting up early and attending Mass, had been admitted free.

After a further more leisurely inspection of the wonders of the mosque, and some fairly futile attempts without flash to photograph it in the very dim light, we turned our attention to the cathedral. Visitors, it is said, often react with indignation at the vandalism, as they see it, which was perpetrated to the unique mosque to permit the construction of the cathedral. The Emperor Charles, as we have seen, called it 'commonplace', but that is scarcely the word that one would now apply to describe this grandiose building, which was built in a mixture of Gothic, Renaissance and baroque styles, and which, were it not overshadowed in every sense by the encircling mosque, would rank in its own right as one of the great cathedrals of Europe.

Close by the mosque is a very familiar street, 'La Calleja de les Flores', the 'Little Alley of Flowers', familiar because its picture appears on all the publicity brochures for Cordoba. Consequently it was thronged with enthusiastic photographers, ourselves included. From the top end of the alley one can get a perfect picture of the cathedral tower rising majestically in the background above the masses of colourful blooms which give the alley its name.

Like Seville, Cordoba has its Alcazar. Internally, apart from some fine and unexpected Roman mosaics, the rooms are less exciting than those of Seville. Outside we risked a slightly hazardous climb to the top of the battlements. 'Only for the nimble,' says one guide book, but these two Saga veterans experienced no particular problems. We were rewarded with a splendid panorama of Cordoba with its old Roman bridge in the foreground. This bridge was built shortly after Caesar's decisive defeat of the forces of Pompey at the battle of Munda, now Montilla, only a few kilometres from Cordoba. Suitably restored and reinforced by the Moors, the bridge still copes with the traffic of the twentieth century.

Without question the great glory of the Alcazar of Cordoba is its superb gardens. I have tended already to wax eloquent over the gardens of Andalucia, but really should have reserved some of my superlatives for these. In addition to all the familiar delights of other gardens of Andalucia, they even include a vegetable garden which is claimed to have been in constant production from the time of the Caliphs! Another unusual feature is groups of modern sculpture. One of these, positioned prominently at one end of the gardens, was of particular interest to the Americans in our party. It represents Ferdinand and Isabella receiving Christopher Columbus and presenting him with his commission to go and discover the New World. The Americans were naturally fascinated, but seemed also more than happy to be discovering for themselves in Andalucia some of the beauties of the Old World from which Columbus set out to discover theirs. These superb gardens, we noticed, are floodlit on summer evenings and open to the public from 10 pm to 1 am. All very Spanish! This has heightened our appreciation ever since of Manuel de Falla's 'Nights in the Gardens of Spain', which in the third movement presents a musical picture of the gardens of Cordoba.

And so, on to Granada, the climax, the grand finale of our tour of Andalucia. It was appropriate in many ways that we should come last of all to Granada. First conquered by the Moors in 711, Granada flourished for almost seven centuries as the wealthiest and most sophisticated city in the Iberian peninsula. Its surrender by the sultan Boabdil to the forces of Ferdinand and Isabella marked the final completion of the 'reconquista' and the end of Moorish power in Spain.

The Catholic monarchs, overjoyed by the final victory of the Christians, decided quickly that they would wish in due course to be buried on the site of their victory. So our first visit was to the cathedral, once again erected over a demolished mosque, another vast building in the Renaissance style, which would be of compelling interest were it not totally outshone, artistically and historically, by the adjoining 'Capilla Real'. This Chapel Royal is the monarchs' mausoleum. In a palatial shrine, inevitably enclosed by a fabulous wrought-iron grille, their tombs stand side by side along with those of their children, Philip the Handsome and the ill-fated Joanna the Mad.

Royal insignia of every kind, banners, coats of arms, statues, initials, are all worked into the decorations not only of the Capilla itself, but also of much of the rest of the cathedral. Many European cathedrals boast a treasury, often located in the sacristy with an extra charge for admission. Few of these can compare with the sacristy of Granada Cathedral. In addition to the usual precious ecclesiastical silverware, one can admire the crown and sceptre of Isabella, her priceless personal jewels and the sword of Ferdinand. Finally there is the queen's private art collection, including some masterpieces of Memling, the Dutch painter whose work we had so much enjoyed in the galleries of Bruges in Belgium.

However, the greatest glory of Granada, some would say of Andalucia, is the Alhambra. Part fortress, part palace, it has excited the boundless admiration of writers and travellers over many centuries. As early as 1494 the German Jeronimo Munzer wrote, 'There is nothing like it in Europe; it is all so magnificent, so majestic, so exquisitely fashioned, that looking at it, one cannot be sure that one is not in Paradise.'

The Alhambra has the advantage of a splendid site on the top of a hill that dominates the whole of the city and looks across a great plain to the snowcapped mountains of the Sierra Nevada on the far horizon. Our guide swept us briskly through a series of superbly decorated chambers, each one of which would have rewarded a good hour's contemplation. Consequently one has a somewhat blurred recollection of endless magnificence — golden mosaics, horseshoe arches, incredibly slender columns, ornamental pools and fountains, and walls covered in superbly intricate abstract designs.

From all these architectural and ornamental wonders three rooms stand out particularly in our memories, aided no doubt by the colour slides that have kept our memories fresh. The first is the Ambassadors' Hall, with every inch of the walls covered with intricate inscriptions and mazy patterns, and topped by a sensational carved wooden ceiling. Our American friends were again fascinated to learn that it was in this hall that Columbus first outlined to Ferdinand his hare-brained schemes for discovering a new world across the ocean.

The second is the Court of Myrtles, a large wide-open oblong space, edged with the myrtle bushes from which it takes its name. There is a fountain at each end and a narrow central pool in between which reflects uncannily in its waters the remarkable architectural symmetry of the buildings which surround it.

And finally, the famous Lion Court. This wonderfully elegant and spacious court is surrounded by an arcade of horseshoe arches resting on no less than 124 incredibly slender white marble columns, some singly, some in pairs. In the centre is the beautiful low-lying sprinkling fountain supported by 12 lions carved in black marble. We really felt that we could understand Jeronimo Munzer's illusions of Paradise.

However, there is just one incongruous jarring note that has to be mentioned in any totally honest appraisal of the Alhambra. Readers will recall, I hope, the scathing remarks of the emperor Charles V regarding the Christian vandalisation of the Mosque at Cordoba. He seems to have had no compunction, however, about doing a very similar job on the Alhambra at Granada, whereby he built himself a grandiose, Italianate palace in its very heart.

Late in the afternoon we moved up the nearby Hill of the Sun to the Generaliffe, the sultans' summer residence, which, unlike the Alhambra, which is ochre red in colour, is gleaming white. By now we were tending to take for granted the sumptuousness of Moorish decoration. In fact, the main wonders of the Generaliffe are not so much the building and its decoration as the incredible gardens found in nooks and crannies all over the place. An irrigation channel flows through the middle of the main garden and feeds various pools, fountains and jets of water which are all fringed with myrtles, laurels and orange trees.

Despite all the superlatives I have lavished on other Moorish gardens, I think that we would have to agree with the verdict of the guide book which pronounces the gardens of the Generaliffe as 'probably the most magnificent in Spain'. We had detached ourselves from Jack and Rina and our American friends and were enjoying a leisurely stroll in these idyllic surroundings when we had a mild panic. We had lost track of time and suddenly realised that the gardens were closing, and we had to make a mad dash to reach the gates before they were locked for the night.

Romantic though it might have been, I don't think that we would have relished spending an unscheduled 'Night in the Gardens of Spain', even in the most magnificent of them all!

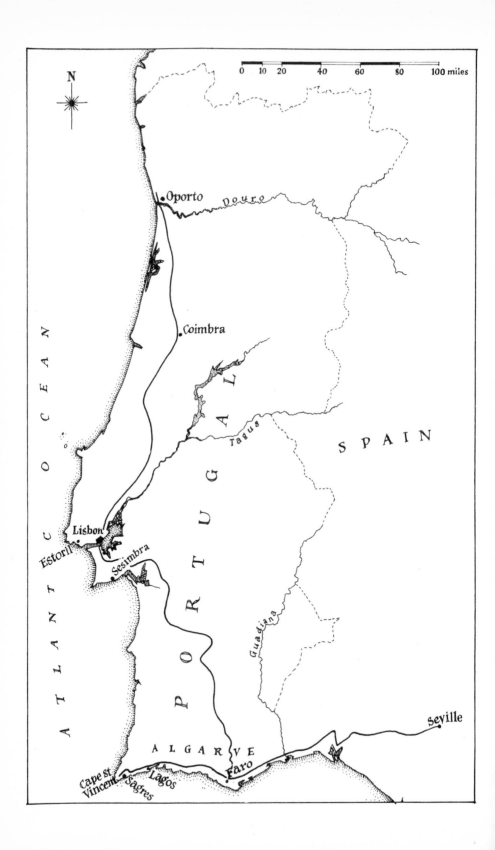

CHAPTER EIGHT

Portugal–Lisbon and the Algarve

We have developed a pleasant habit over the years of passing the time on the journey home from one holiday by discussing ideas for the next. Our immensely enjoyable Saga tour of Andalucia, the furthermost part of Spain, understandably stimulated our interest in the possibility of exploring Portugal, another distant part of the Iberian peninsula. So distant, in fact, that we observed with some amusement that the proposed itinerary in the Saga brochure included Cape St Vincent, known to the ancients as 'O Fin do Mundo', the 'End of the World'. Not quite that these days perhaps, but still far enough away to deter ageing pensioners like us from tackling the journey by car. So we readily and with pleasurable anticipation accepted Saga's invitation to join their two-centre holiday in Portugal.

The two centres were Estoril on the coast near Lisbon and Lagos on the coast of the Algarve. Estoril had obviously been selected for the first half of the holiday as a convenient base for the exploration of Lisbon. We found, however, that it also had a certain minor interest of its own, and in particular a strange faded elegance due to the fact that in the latter part of the nineteenth century it had been a favourite refuge for dispossessed nobility of various nations and even abdicated monarchs. These days Estoril's proudest possession appeared to be its large casino, offering tourists a remarkably wide selection of ways in which to lose their money, We studiously ignored its blandishments, but found the casino gardens, which were open to the public, a pleasant place in which to stroll amongst colourful rose beds, bougainvillaea and hibiscus before dinner in the evening.

The most important place in Estoril for us was its small railway station, from which a frequent service transported us into the centre of Lisbon in less than half an hour. We had previously visited almost every other capital city of western Europe, but had a feeling that Lisbon would be quite different from any of the others. For one thing it had acquired a certain mystique for us Second World War veterans, as almost the only western capital that was never involved in the war. (Madrid, of course, was another; but then we were expecting from week to week that Franco would bring Spain into the war on the side of Germany and Italy.) There were always intriguing rumours during the war about Lisbon as the neutral port where spies and shady diplomats from both sides were arranging secret rendezvous to influence the course of the war. The sort of place, in fact, where a few centuries earlier, Rosemary's Hartang von Kluck would have been in his element.

Again Lisbon is one of the few capital cities of Europe which is a major port, where the presence of the sea is all pervasive, and where a salty tang of the sea is always in the air. The city slopes gently upwards from the shore of the great River Tagus, and from almost every vantage point ships, wharves and docks can be seen for miles around. Dominating this scene is the giant suspension bridge, the longest in Europe, built in 1966 and high enough to allow the tallest passenger liner to pass safely beneath.

Apart from the river and the sea, the main attractions of Lisbon are its spacious and elegant squares and gardens and its magnificent tree-lined avenues of which the finest, the Avenida da Liberdade, is considered to rival even the Champs Elysées of Paris. It was not always so. On the Feast of All Saints, 1 November 1755, a catastrophe of almost unimaginable proportions struck the city in the shape of a gigantic earthquake, which devastated most of Lisbon and much of the rest of Portugal. Survivors described how at first there was a low rumble, then the earth heaved up, then down and sideways. The River Tagus seemed to boil, they said, before it swept over the city in a huge tidal wave. It is estimated that between 40,000 and 50,000 people were killed, many of them when the churches, where they were attending Mass, collapsed on top of them. Western Europe perhaps had not experienced so great a natural disaster since AD 79 when that totally unexpected eruption of Vesuvius completely obliterated the towns of Pompeii and Herculaneum.

There was one area of the city which miraculously escaped the full force of the disaster, Belem, several miles to the west where the king, Jose I, and the royal court and the king's chief minister, the future Marquis of Pombal, were in residence. The king gave Pombal virtually dictatorial powers, first of all to restore some semblance of order, and then to rebuild the shattered city. This he proceeded to do on wholly revolutionary lines. It was an early and highly successful example of town planning. The spacious squares and wide tree-lined boulevards that we were admiring were the main features of Pombal's reconstruction of the city.

The finest of these squares is down by the river, and has three sides built in the gracious style that has come to be known appropriately as Pombaline, with the fourth side completely open to the river. It is hard to discover what the name of this square really is. Its official name is apparently 'Praco de Comercio', but it is invariably referred to by the Portuguese as 'Terreiro de Paco', and by all English speakers as 'Black Horse Square'. The rider on the black horse is King Jose I, but even that name is now scarcely appropriate, since the king and his horse, rather like Napoléon, as we noticed on the Route Napoléon, have weathered over the years to a somewhat sickly shade of green.

An impressive statue of Pombal himself dominates another square which is actually circular rather than square, and from this the majestic Avenida da Liberdade, the imitation Champs Elysées, extends a full mile to yet another fine square, the Rossio, where a rather antiquated elevator designed by a Monsieur Eiffel (who did a rather more famous and elegant job in Paris), takes one to an upper part of the city. A short way from the top of Eiffel's elevator we came upon a somewhat chilling sight. A fourteenth century Carmelite church stands roofless, with its giant Gothic pillars open to the sky. The church was deliberately left in this devastated state after the earthquake of 1 November 1755, to be a permanent memorial of that dark day in Portuguese history.

The spacious squares and elegant boulevards which contribute so notably to the attractions of Lisbon are further enhanced by a feature that we had never seen anywhere else. Black and white mosaics in formal chequered patterns cover almost every inch of every square and every pavement, and add a most unusual extra dimension of beauty to the central part of the city. While aesthetically delightful, the small granite squares that make up the mosaics present certain pitfalls for the unwary. Some ladies of our party, unwisely shod in high-heeled shoes, found the gaps between the pieces occasionally treacherous. An indomitable old friend of mine who regularly takes his handicapped wife on holiday abroad in a wheelchair, told me that these beautiful pavements of Lisbon were quite the most hazardous and tiring that he had ever had to negotiate.

As mentioned earlier, the earthquake that destroyed most of Lisbon and rocked the greater part of Portugal, miraculously spared the Belem district, a few kilometres from the centre of the city. This whole area is something of a paradise for an historically-minded tourist. It contains at least three monuments of major importance, and is unquestionably worth a full day's exploration to itself. Fortunately it was conveniently accessible on the electric railway from our base in Estoril.

The most important of these monuments of Belem is the Jeronimos monastery. It was founded by King Manuel in 1502, and is designed in a peculiarly Portuguese version of Gothic known as Manueline. Astonishingly slender, soaring pillars are decorated their whole length in complicated motifs which include ropes, fish, shells, coral, anchors and in fact almost anything else connected with the sea. The monastery is reckoned the supreme masterpiece of this Manueline form of architecture. Its cloisters are even more extravagant and exotic and adorned with even more fantastic decoration. The interior of this remarkable monastery church contains the tombs of many kings, queens and princes, and most striking of all, the tombs of Vasco da Gama, the discoverer of the sea route to India, and of Camoes, the greatest Portuguese poet. The boundless magnificence of this remarkable building was popularly said to have been paid for out of pepper! It was indeed financed, as were many other great undertakings at this period, from the enormous wealth that poured into Lisbon from the trade in spices and the riches of the Orient during the period of 'The Great Discoveries'.

Which brings us to the next notable point of interest in the Belem quarter of Lisbon, the Monument to the Discoveries. This striking and hugely photogenic piece of modern sculpture was erected by the shore of the River Tagus to celebrate the five hundreth anniversary in 1960 of the death of Prince Henry the Navigator. It represents the crew of a ship with Prince Henry himself pointing the way forward to a crowd of sea captains, navigators, priests, poets and supporters of every kind. The monument is surrounded by one of the finest of Lisbon's black and white mosaic pavements in the form of a map of the world featuring the lands and seas that the Prince inspired his countrymen to discover.

It soon became obvious to us, both in Lisbon and even more so later in Lagos on the Algarve, that Prince Henry is definitely Portugal's favourite son. My historian wife was particularly fascinated by all the homage paid to him. Any readers who have the similar good fortune to have an historian in the family will be familiar with an engaging but sometimes irritating habit that they have. When asked for information on some historical subject, they cheerfully reply, 'Sorry, not my period!' However, Prince Henry *was* Rosemary's period; she even informed me that he had English connections and was, in fact, the grandson of Shakespeare's 'Old John of Gaunt, time-honoured Lancaster'.

The scale of the achievements of Prince Henry and the explorers and sea captains that he gathered around himself, can scarcely be exaggerated. The advances in navigation, astronomy, cartography and ship design that he inspired enabled sailors to venture ever further into the unknown, until finally Vasco da Gama discovered the sea route to the Indies. In all, these intrepid adventurers from this small country discovered in the fifteenth century nearly two-thirds of the inhabited globe, an achievement, it has been suggested, as tremendous for the fifteenth century as putting a man on the moon in the twentieth.

Nearby is a third reminder of Lisbon's nautical past, another Manueline monument known as the Belem Tower. Beautifully proportioned and elaborately decorated, it has been described as looking like an ivory chess-piece. Its elegance is deceptive, however; it was designed first and foremost as a powerfully equipped defence position against potential enemies attacking the city from the river.

Finally, Belem had yet another, but very different showpiece for our interest and entertainment, the National Coach Museum. This most unusual museum houses no less than 74 state coaches which, not surprisingly, is claimed to be the largest collection of such vehicles in the world. Most of them are incredibly ornate, many adorned with the gold and riches that the sea captains brought home from Brazil and other new Portuguese possessions. Many are of great historical interest, including the coach in which both Edward VII and Elizabeth II drove along the great avenues of Lisbon on their state visits to the capital of Britain's oldest ally.

If this coach museum is the most unusual of the many museums that Lisbon, like most big cities, is able to display for the benefit of its tourists, the most rewarding, we thought, was undoubtedly the Gulbenkian. This museum was luxuriously purpose-built to house the priceless art collection bequeathed to Lisbon by the multimillionaire oil tycoon of that name, and most deservedly wins Michelin's rare three-star accolade. The Gulbenkian seems to house nothing but masterpieces. Superb examples of Greek and Roman art, Chinese pottery and Persian carpets accompany some of the finest paintings of Rembrandt, Turner, Rubens, Gainsborough and the French Impressionists. When we were there, the entrance fee for all this magnificence was a derisory 20 pence. No doubt it is a lot more now.

We had one wet day during our week in Lisbon in late October, but the rain unexpectedly provided us with one of the strangest and most memorable experiences of all our travels around Europe. From every high point in the city, as I mentioned earlier, one has a view of the River Tagus and the mighty suspension bridge that spans it. Equally visible from most viewpoints is a towering statue of Christ in Majesty or Christ the King, which overlooks the city from a hill on the other side of the river. The statue was erected in 1968 as a mark of gratitude for Portugal having remained at peace throughout both world wars.

On the wet day in question we were scheduled to make an

expedition to Sesimbra, a pretty fishing village, and to the mountains of the Serra da Arribida. The route lay across the suspension bridge, with a planned stop for the ascent of the statue of Christ the King. However, the clouds were so thick and low and the rain so heavy that the statue was completely invisible, and most members of the party didn't even trouble to leave the coach. The few of us who did were informed by our local guide (who also didn't trouble to leave the coach), that there was a lift to take us most of the way followed by 'a few steps'. We would then emerge on to the platform on which the statue is supported by four massive pillars.

At the entrance to the elevator there was an impressive notice which read, 'This is the shrine of the national gratitude; please go up as a pilgrim not as a tourist'. As we emerged from the lift, we found that it was necessary to proceed in single file up the 'few steps' which turned out to be 75 in number (we counted them). This final ascent was led by Tommy, an 85-year-old retired headmaster, who had mentioned casually the previous evening that he had recently undergone a hip replacement operation. Progress was agonisingly slow, but with dogged determination Tommy eventually reached the platform, closely followed by the rest of us who certainly by now felt more like pilgrims than tourists. It was then that we pilgrims beheld an awe-inspiring apparition. There before us stood Christ in Majesty, clearly but eerily visible *above* the clouds. A quite remarkable and memorable experience.

After that, Sesimbra in the rain was something of an anticlimax. The supposedly pretty village was largely lost in the clouds, but we were at least able to inspect the great covered fish market, all smelly and slippery with a most wonderful assortment of monsters from the deep. Most notable amongst these were two colossal tuna fish, each large enough to feed a regiment for a year. The return journey to Lisbon over the mountainous Serra da Arrabida, also completely lost in the clouds, was slightly unnerving. It was by now quite dark as we approached the city and gradually descended to the Tagus bridge. Then the weather suddenly cleared, and we were able to enjoy striking views of the city's many handsome monuments all brilliantly and attractively floodlit.

Although Lisbon's many places of interest are spread over a

fairly wide area, we found it a relatively easy city to explore on foot, with the help of occasional buses and taxis. Taxis, in particular, are plentiful and cheap. We found it necessary, for instance, to take a taxi to visit the castle which is on top of the highest hill. It was actually founded by the Moors, and served to remind us that Portugal as well as Spain was occupied by Moors for several centuries. The castle is surrounded by extensive gardens of the Andalucian type with tropical plants, pools and exotic birds. Within easy reach is the cathedral and the Church of St Anthony who, we were surprised to learn, was born on this site and not in Italian Padua as we had always imagined.

Having dismissed our taxi we then walked downhill through the Alfama district which, like Belem, escaped the worst effects of the earthquake, and therefore, unlike the rest of Lisbon, is a veritable warren of narrow medieval streets. We were warned that this area is a favourite haunt of muggers and bag-snatchers, but happily none of our party experienced any untoward incidents which would justify this reputation. We also found that most things that a tourist wants were agreeably cheap in Lisbon. It was helpful, too, that English was widely spoken in shops and hotels, which was just as well, since Portuguese seemed to us quite the least comprehensible of the Romance languages, with a puzzling and bewildering number of shushing sounds.

There is no doubt that Lisbon is a paradise for fish eaters; the ichthyophagous can feast on sea bass, swordfish, bream, tuna steaks and, my own favourite, very substantial fish soup, which all make a pleasant change from the routine cod and haddock back home. Not forgetting the sardines, which to us had previously meant those tiny fish crammed into small tins. When we ordered sardines for a snack one day, we were presented with half a dozen each, mostly about a foot in length.

So on to Lagos in the Algarve, for the second leg of this two centre holiday. The Algarve, of course, has become extremely popular with British holidaymakers, mainly because of its ideal climate in both summer and winter. The official brochure in fact claims that its winter temperatures are higher than the Spanish Costas, and that its annual hours of sunshine exceed everywhere else on the northern side of the Mediterranean. Our hotel was a little distance outside Lagos (incidentally pronounced Lagosh in the shushing manner mentioned above), and there was a courtesy coach available to take us into the town. This luxury hotel was set amidst gardens with palm trees, hibiscus, bougainvillaea and giant geraniums, all mostly in full bloom. We had to keep reminding ourselves that we were actually holidaying at the beginning of November.

Lagos itself is a most attractive little fishing port, certainly quiet and peaceful in November, though apparently, like the rest of the Algarve, it is swarming with tourists in the season. We found that it has a quite remarkable Church of St Anthony, known locally as the 'Golden Chapel', an extreme example of extravagant baroque with literally every inch of the interior smothered in elaborate golden decoration. We were told that only the altar survived the earthquake of 1755, which devastated this part of Portugal no less than Lisbon. However, pious citizens then restored the golden wonder exactly as it had been before. Attached to the chapel is a small museum which contains a rare medley of local crafts and folklore, but also some fine Roman mosaics. Whenever we paused briefly in our progress round the museum to admire some particular exhibit, a pleasant young girl attendant would unobtrusively materialise, and in commendable English politely explain the exhibit's particular significance. Another splendid feature of this unusual chapel and museum is that admission is free to OAPs.

Lagos has seen some stirring times. It was founded by the Romans (hence the unexpected mosaics in the museum), and was developed as a major port by the Moors during their period of occupation. It reached its zenith during the Age of the Discoveries, when it was the port from which most of those newly-designed caravelles set out on their hazardous journeys, while its workshops were responsible for the construction of the ships themselves. Most appropriately, therefore, in the central square is a fine statue of the inspiring genius himself, Prince Henry the Navigator. Not far away, however, there is a sad reminder that this great age of exploration, which he and his disciples pioneered, also had its darker side. A small arcaded fifteenth century building was the first slave market in Europe. It is said that people came from miles around to gaze upon this sensational new phenomenon — black men from Africa.

We were naturally looking forward with keen anticipation to that excursion to 'The End of the World', 'O Fin do Mundo', otherwise known as Cape St Vincent, the most south-westerly point of Europe, where the continent first encounters the full force of the Atlantic Ocean. On the edge of a sheer cliff some 250 feet above the sea there now stands one of the most powerful lighthouses in the world, which can cast a beam some 60 miles out to sea. We were able to climb up to the platform (but without Tommy this time!), immediately below the giant lamp with its huge lenses, that were renewed in 1982.

As we clung to the rail of the windswept platform gazing unsteadily over the seemingly limitless expanse of the ocean, we could well understand how the ancients believed that this was indeed the end of the world. Not so, however, as we have seen, the far-sighted Henry the Navigator, who around 1415 established at nearby Sagres his renowned school of navigation, where he assembled the leading explorers, sea captains and experts in the various maritime sciences. Not much of Henry's school now remains; it was yet another victim of that disastrous earthquake of 1755. Part of what survived has been converted into a youth hostel, an appropriate use perhaps of this dramatic, desolate spot where the likes of Vasco da Gama, Magellan, Diaz and Cabral (the discoverer of Brazil), and also, some say, Christopher Columbus, found the inspiration that fired the imagination of the youth of the fifteenth and sixteenth centuries.

A large area of the site immediately in front of the former school was lightly excavated a few years ago and a giant mariner's compass was revealed, which presumably was used by the pupils for their navigational exercises. Key points on the compass were marked out by 'azulejos', the traditional blue tiles of both Spain and Portugal. However, so many of them were later stolen by tourists as souvenirs, that the remainder were removed for safety to a museum in Lisbon, and replaced by common or garden stones. Rosemary and I (and especially Rosemary), found the whole area uniquely fascinating as having been the prime source and inspiration of so many of the greatest historic developments and discoveries of medieval times.

Against all this background of the tremendous achievements of the Christian Portuguese it would have been easy to forget that the Moors were in control of this part of Portugal for several centuries. We were reminded of this by an excursion to Silves, the one-time capital of Moorish Portugal, and a city then of 30,000 inhabitants. There is now not much to see; the ravages of time, and particularly of 1755, have left only the red limestone walls of the Alcazaba and a badly damaged Christian cathedral.

We were steadily discovering that there are many agreeable aspects of Saga holidays that we had not expected. One is that these holidays often include in the programme an evening of folk music of the area concerned. In Andalucia it had naturally been flamenco. In Portuguese Lagos the entertainment took the form of song and dance by an enthusiastic and extremely well-drilled troupe of juvenile dancers and musicians, some of them very young indeed. At the end of the performance there was naturally prolonged and well-deserved applause, whereupon the performers invited the members of the audience to join them in a final romp. I have a treasured and abiding recollection of a tiny little girl gravely approaching Tommy, our 85-year-old (he who had been first up the statue of Christ the King), and with exquisite courtesy inviting him to partner her in the dance. He, scorning the discrepancy of nearly 80 years, gallantly responded with alacrity and escorted her into the merry throng. As for myself, I am ashamed to confess that I was a coward and quietly dodged the column.

I cannot resist recalling an even more memorable evening's folk music on another Saga holiday, in the beautiful Polish city of Cracow. I'm afraid that there is no chapter in this book on that tour of Poland, simply because it took place immediately before the Polish revolution, and our impressions would be out of date and potentially misleading. For even more obvious reasons there is no chapter on Yugoslavia, where we enjoyed two immensely rewarding and entirely peaceful holidays, which make the subsequent tragic events utterly unbelievable.

That evening of folk music in Cracow was quite unforgettable, and since music transcends politics, similar performances must surely be continuing. We were intrigued to begin with when the concert was advertised as being presented by seven sisters. Our local guide assured us that this was literally true. On our arrival at the venue we found that only five sisters had in fact turned up, but a compère with tolerable English explained that the numbers were being made up by a boyfriend — and Mother! These sisters simply had everything; they were all beautiful, and immensely talented and versatile musicians. One expects folk music to be performed with a certain rustic simplicity; this performance was of a uniformly professional standard.

It was easy to guess at one source at least of the sisters' musical talents; Mother, also slim and beautiful despite her numerous progeny, was clearly an expert instrumentalist herself. Nor was it the end of the line, as soon became evident. The compère seemed to feel that he ought to apologise more fully for the absence of two of the seven sisters. So he made a speech in his very basic English. The two absent sisters, he explained, were very sad at their inability to be with us. Then there was an excruciating pause, as he struggled desperately for the right words. 'They cannot be here,' he finally pronounced, 'because they are giving birth!'

I have already said that another unexpected bonus of Saga holidays is the quality of the company, like-minded veterans with a lifetime's accumulated wisdom and experience. We were always surprised how quickly we made new and lasting friendships. For instance, on the Polish trip that I have just mentioned, we met Jack and Mary, with whom we have kept happily in touch ever since, and many others on holidays that I shall be writing about later. Portugal was special, however, because it was there that we met Andrew!

Andrew and his wife Connie dined with us every evening during that fortnight. A favourite topic of conversation over dinner is often previous Saga holidays that one has enjoyed. I happened to mention the tour of classical Greece and its special interest for me. This produced an astonishing response from Andrew. It quickly became clear that he was a genuine amateur classical scholar, amateur in the best sense of the word, one with a deep love of his subject. Without any formal qualification of any kind, Andrew had amassed an immense knowledge of the civilisations of ancient Greece and Rome. We had many fascinating conversations over our post-prandial coffees in the lounge.

That was not the end of the story. On our return to Britain (I had nearly said England, but Andrew is from Scotland and proud of it), he favoured me with the first of a long series of lengthy letters. These are invariably replete with his deep and wide-ranging knowledge of ancient history, literature and philosophy. They always modestly and quite mistakenly defer to my greater academic expertise when, in fact, he frequently leaves me floundering hopelessly out of my depth.

Andrew recently celebrated his eightieth birthday. His devoted family planned to surprise him with a specially composed 'birthday book'. His son, aware of the afore-mentioned unusual correspondence, kindly invited me to contribute. I was more than happy to comply, and thought it appropriate to write a part of my piece in Latin. In case Andrew had any difficulty with the translation, I surreptitiously supplied his son with a 'crib'. I gather that my contribution was much appreciated by the recipient.

I hope that I don't need to apologise for this lengthy digression. If nothing else, it illustrates the fact that in booking for a Saga fortnight, one is often getting much more than just that for one's money.

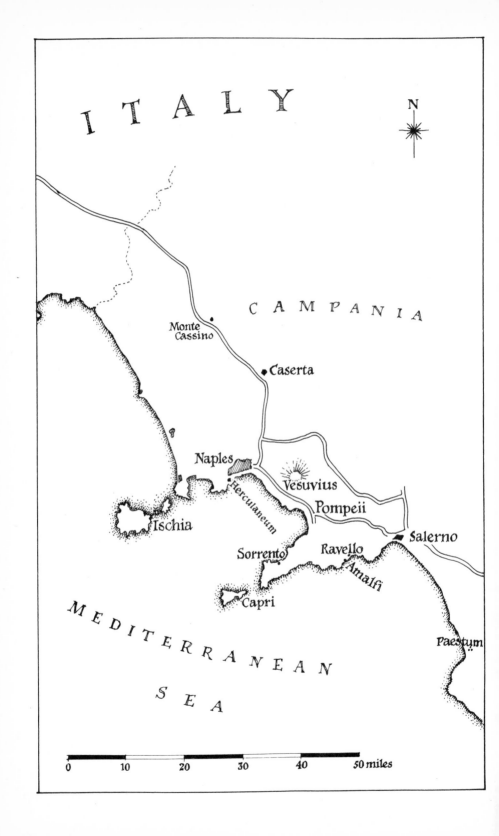

ITALY

CAMPANIA

N

Monte
Cassino

Caserta

Naples

Vesuvius

Herculaneum

Pompeii

Ischia

Salerno

Sorrento

Ravello

Amalfi

Capri

Paestum

MEDITERRANEAN

SEA

0   10   20   30   40   50 miles

CHAPTER NINE

Southern Italy

'Anyone fascinated by "The Glory That Was Greece" and "The Grandeur That Was Rome" can enjoy a unique sample of both in one and the same place by visiting Paestum in Southern Italy.'

Thus I introduced my first article in the Catholic weekly, *The Universe*, after our return from Paestum. Yet at an earlier stage, when Paul Bach of Saga Holidays rang me and invited me to try their holiday at Paestum, I had to confess to my shame that I had never heard of the place. 'What,' he said, 'it's right up your street, it's a famous classical site!'

However, after I had studied the literature about Paestum I felt a little better. I discovered that nobody at all had heard of the place for something like 900 years, from AD 871, when it was finally abandoned by its inhabitants, until the late eighteenth century, when it was accidentally rediscovered during the construction of a road down the west coast of southern Italy. The roadmakers happened to discern some strange, impressive columns concealed among thick woodland in a deserted malarial swamp. It was actually not until 1952 that systematic exploration of the site was undertaken.

So my wife and I gazed almost with incredulity on three magnificent Greek temples dating from the fifth and sixth centuries BC. They stand in 50 acres of a green and pleasant 'zona archeologica'. They are surrounded by the remains of the important Roman city that later grew up around them, and are encircled by several miles of genuine Roman walls. All three temples are in a remarkable state of preservation. Since they were lost to sight for all those centuries, they have escaped the looting and vandalism that has often been the fate of similar sites elsewhere, which have been pillaged for their valuable building materials.

The finest of the three, the Temple of Poseidon, is claimed by experts to be the most complete major temple to have survived from the greatest period of Greek architecture, and to be in every respect, except sheer size (it is slightly smaller), superior even to the Parthenon in Athens. And whereas to view the Parthenon on the Acropolis in Athens one has to survive the heavily polluted atmosphere, and struggle up the Propylaea with hordes of other tourists at any time of the year, here we were in Paestum in mid-September with the whole lovely verdant area virtually to ourselves.

Why, you may well ask, if these ruins are so important and so magnificent, are they so relatively little known? The answer is one of the strangest stories in the history of archaeology. Paestum, the Roman version of Poseidonia, named after the Greek god of the sea, was one of many colonies founded by the Greeks around 600 BC in the area of southern Italy later known, for this reason, as 'Magna Graecia'.

About this time the Greeks of the mainland were planting colonies all around the Mediterranean region. Many of them are major cities to this day. Naples, some 60 miles north of Paestum, is one of the best known; its Greek name Neapolis meant Newtown. Marseilles in the south of France is another, Syracuse in Sicily and Taranto on the heel of Italy are others. Paestum was colonised from the Greek city of Sybaris, whose inhabitants, notorious for their high living, gave the word 'sybarite' to our language.

Magna Graecia, of course, like the rest of Italy and the Mediterranean area generally, was subsequently absorbed into the Roman Empire. We know that Paestum was a flourishing city in Roman times because it is mentioned by the poets Ovid and Propertius, and especially Virgil who refers to it in his *Georgics* as having fine roses which flowered twice in the year. A well-paved Roman 'via sacra' crosses the site, there is a Roman forum, a gymnasium and half an amphitheatre — only half because the other half is under the modern road and cannot be excavated.

Later the sea receded, however, and the river silted up. As early as the first century BC the Greek writer Strabo tells us that Paestum was already getting a bad name for the malaria-ridden marshland that developed around it. Thereafter the dating is hazy, as the inhabitants progressively withdrew to higher ground above the city. The local guide book says 'The silence of the centuries and the obscurity of the Middle Ages descended upon the city'.

During the systematic excavations that have taken place since 1952, a series of ancient tombs have been discovered, and in 1968 there emerged from one of these some truly sensational frescoes, certainly the finest examples of ancient Greek painting to have survived. Paestum, therefore, can justifiably boast of being the only place in the world to possess first-rate sculpture, architecture *and* painting from the fifth century BC, the golden age of the ancient Greek civilisation.

On a rare wet day during our stay at Paestum, we spent several very rewarding hours in the splendid purpose-built museum that stands just across the road from that bisected amphitheatre. The museum has a superb collection of miscellaneous artefacts from the 'zona archeologica'. One ticket admits to both 'zona' and 'museo', but of course, in accordance with the admirable Italian practice, no charge for OAPs producing a foreign passport.

Far and away the most notable of the museum's many important exhibits are the frescoes from the so-called 'Tomb of the Diver'. The finest of these panels, all with their colours amazingly well-preserved, depicts a naked youth gracefully taking off from a diving board into a blue lake below. It has been suggested that, since the painting comes from a tomb, it may be an allegory of the soul leaving the body.

We could probably have spent our whole fortnight happily pottering around that remarkable 'zona archeologica' and its associated museum, especially since the pleasant hotel, in which we were housed in individual chalets with bougainvillaea wreathed around the doors, was only just across the road from the temples. However, we also knew that Paestum is only 20 miles or so from Salerno, which is at the southern end of the celebrated Amalfi Drive. We remembered that Dr Johnson had said that 'The grand object of travel is to see the coasts of the Mediterranean'. Here was our great opportunity.

Michelin, usually very sparing in his superlatives, says quite simply, 'The corniche road that follows the rocky coast from

Sorrento to Salerno is the finest in Italy'. Italian engineers, who seem to have inherited from their Roman ancestors their legendary skills in road and bridge building, have constructed a remarkable highway that clings to the mountainside high above the sea. Coming from Paestum we obviously traversed it in the opposite direction.

After Salerno the scenery becomes suddenly dramatic. At each bend there are fresh views of precipitous hillsides plunging steeply into the deep blue Mediterranean. It is not a very suitable drive for the nervous, as the coach negotiates endless hairpin bends with sheer cliff faces immediately below. We felt that the driver surely qualified for danger money, but he seemed to regard it as all in a day's work, as he calmly smoked the inevitable cigarette.

We were surprised to observe that, despite the unpromising nature of the terrain and the extreme steepness of the slopes, industrious peasants nevertheless contrive to cultivate the hillsides with lemon and orange trees, olives and figs and hardy flowering shrubs, which temper somewhat the wildness of the scenery, which became ever more spectacular until our first stop at Amalfi itself.

Amalfi, now no more than a picturesque little town, in the Middle Ages was one of the great maritime republics. On a wall near the entrance to the old town is a large ceramic map of this part of the Mediterranean with a Latin inscription, 'Contra hostes fidei semper pugnavit Amalphis' — 'Amalfi has always fought against the enemies of the faith' — a reference presumably to the important part played by the Amalfi navy in transporting crusaders to the Holy Land.

Amalfi's Cathedral of St Andrew has a dramatic situation at the top of a great flight of steps. Its striking façade includes a magnificent portico of coloured marble in intricate designs that are clearly of Moorish inspiration. Even more obviously Moorish is the adjoining 'Cloister of Paradise', which is extremely beautiful and was well worth the entrance fee of 1,000 lire. Much older still are two ancient pillars inside the cathedral which particularly interested our party since they are supposed to have been removed from one of the Greek temples at Paestum.

Along an even more tortuous road six kilometres higher up the mountain stands Ravello. This time our coach clearly was too long for the job, and the driver had to stop frequently and then manoeuvre perilously round the worst of the hairpin bends to a chorus of hooting horns in front and behind. Italian motorists simply cannot bear to be held up even briefly, and in any case enjoy any excuse for making a din. We noticed a team of donkeys for hire by the roadside, and wondered whether they were not a more suitable form of transport in these parts!

At Ravello we found another ancient cathedral, much plainer externally than Amalfi, but with an impressive thirteenth century campanile and a marvellous pulpit decorated with many kinds of fantastic animals. There was clearly a great deal more of interest to see in this immensely picturesque little town which, somewhat unbelievably considering its almost inaccessible situation, had been a flourishing city of more than 30,000 citizens in the Middle Ages. However, we had not a great deal of time, and our guide quite rightly advised that we should concentrate on the historic Villa Rufolo.

This famous residence, the home of several Popes at one time, turned out to have quite the most extravagantly beautiful garden that we had ever had the good fortune to see. In saying that, I am only too aware of the fact that I have already exhausted my repertoire of horticultural superlatives on Monet's wonderful garden at Giverny in France and the gardens of Andalucia in Spain. So perhaps I should invoke the usually prosaic Michelin who for once waxes almost lyrical: 'The eleventh and twelfth century architecture and the gardens make a picture of truly Oriental beauty in which sunlight shimmers, tea-roses bloom and fountains play'.

It is, of course, its sensational situation that gives the garden of the Villa Rufolo its incomparable beauty. From the garden itself, with its gorgeous array of exotic blooms framed in the Moorish elegance of the villa, one looks out upon the jagged peaks of the mountains above, and the deep blue of the Mediterranean a thousand feet below. The composer Wagner evidently shared our enthusiasm for the Villa Rufolo. He actually resided here for a time, and the unsurpassed beauty of the place gave him the inspiration for Klingsor's enchanted garden in his music-drama *Parsifal*.

'Capri, the Island of Dreams, is one of the high spots of international tourism' says the invaluable Michelin, if I may once again call him in evidence. So, on another excursion from Paestum we this time sailed along the Amalfi coast in high anticipation, and incidentally enjoying an infinitely smoother ride than the one we had experienced in the coach on land. Our local guide excitedly pointed out to us from the boat a luxurious villa gleaming white on the cliffside, the home of Sophia Loren. Viewed from the sea, it was not at all clear how the great lady ever got in or out.

On arrival at Marina Grande on Capri we were transported in minibuses; nothing larger, apparently, is permitted on the island. Our minibus hurtled up and down the steep, twisting roads in rather alarming fashion, past other minibuses hurtling in the opposite direction. The guide, however, was reassuring; he helpfully remarked that only rarely does one go over the edge into the sea. We did arrive safely at the celebrated Villa Michele, the home of Axel Munthe, the Swedish doctor and author of *The Story of San Michele*. The house is elaborately and luxuriously furnished, with an emphasis on copies of ancient Greek and Roman statuary and seventeenth and eighteenth century furnishings. However, the main interest at Villa San Michele is again (dare I mention it?), the quite superb garden, affording a magnificent panorama over much of this uniquely beautiful island.

'A bit better than Rochdale, isn't it?' remarked an elderly gentleman, a complete stranger, who sat down beside us on a bench overlooking Marina Piccola and the former home of Gracie Fields. Indeed, the incomparable beauty of the scenery all around us made it easy to understand why the rich and famous, from the Emperors Augustus and Tiberius onwards, have opted to live on this island paradise.

We were reminded indeed that the Emperor Tiberius deserted Rome for Capri for the last 10 years of his life, and yet contrived to keep effective control of the huge Roman Empire, a fact illustrated by a famous line of the poet Juvenal, 'Verbosa et grandis epistola venit a Capreis' — 'A huge wordy letter came from Capri' — and was sufficient to bring about the downfall of his all-powerful minister Sejanus. Unfortunately there was not time to visit the remains of the Villa Jovis, the palace of Tiberius. There are many weird legends about the extraordinary life-style pursued here by the

Emperor, of which there are powerful hints in the writings of the historians Tacitus and Suetonius. A more interesting and wholesome tradition claims that it was on Capri that the Emperor Tiberius first received word of the strange happenings in Jerusalem, and the crucifixion of a certain Jesus Christ.

We had only time for a few hours in Sorrento, that other earthly paradise of Neapolitan song and legend, but we were able to explore some of the narrow streets and the broad squares lined with palm trees. This admittedly superficial inspection gave us the impression that Sorrento was less brash and commercialised than we had expected. We visited two fine churches; it was Saturday and both evidently had weddings about to happen. The sheer quantity of flowers in each reminded us rather of the marquees at the Southport Flower Show. In one of these churches a trio of piano, violin and cello was having trouble rehearsing Schubert's 'Ave Maria'.

Sorrento, of course, owes its fame to its superb situation high on a headland, affording a vast panorama over the Bay of Naples, but it would appear a less than ideal resort for sand lovers and sun worshippers. We were amused to observe that the latter, owing to the shortage of beach, were obliged to make do with deckchairs on wooden platforms built out into the sea on stilts.

Amalfi, Ravello, Sorrento, Capri. Almost a mini-Grand Tour! We felt that Dr. Johnson would have thoroughly approved! Yet there were two more optional excursions from this Saga holiday at Paestum that we knew we simply could not afford to miss. Some years previously we had made a special trip to London to visit at the Royal Academy the 'Pompeii AD 79' exhibition, and had found it quite awe-inspiring. Now here was an opportunity to see the real thing for ourselves.

The beautifully illustrated catalogue to that memorable exhibition introduced the subject as follows. 'On the morning of the 24th of August AD 79, the long dormant volcano of Vesuvius blew up, and by the evening of that day the two flourishing towns of Pompeii and Herculaneum were dead, already half buried by the rain of ash, pumice and volcanic mud beneath which they were to lie entombed for more than 16 centuries.' A contemporary witness, the Roman writer Pliny the Younger, referred to 'a catastrophe which destroyed the loveliest regions of the earth, a fate shared by whole cities and their peoples'.

Few natural disasters in European history (Lisbon perhaps in 1755 was in the same category), can have equalled the sheer horror of that sudden eruption of a volcano which had been presumed for centuries to be entirely extinct. There had been no previous activity in recorded history. Farms and vineyards clothed the slopes of the mountain, and the surrounding area had become a holiday resort for the rich and famous. Pliny himself narrowly escaped with his life, and his even more famous uncle was killed along with tens of thousands of unsuspecting citizens.

Pompeii was overwhelmed by burning ash and pumice to a depth of over 20 feet. Herculaneum was submerged in a sea of mud and molten lava over 60 feet deep. These cities were literally wiped off the map; they simply ceased to exist. Over the following centuries nature took over, and the forgotten sites became rich agricultural land. The buried cities were only rediscovered as recently as the eighteenth century.

At first excavation was no more than haphazard treasure hunting, and many of the notable finds from that period can be inspected today in the National Museum at Naples. Scientific excavation began only in the late nineteenth century, when a technique was developed of restoring the buildings, where possible, as they stood, surrounded by gardens much as they would have appeared before that fatal day in AD 79.

If the London exhibition had been awe-inspiring, it was naturally nothing compared to the real thing on the ground. More interesting even than the impressive public buildings, forum, temples, baths and amphitheatre, are the hundreds of ordinary private houses, particularly those in Herculaneum. Here the solidified mud has effectively preserved even the woodwork of three-storey houses, complete with their furniture, ornaments and floors in intricate patterns of mosaic.

In Pompeii the ash and pumice proved easier to remove than the solidified mud at Herculaneum, and revealed some stunning wall paintings, which it is difficult to credit are nearly 2,000 years old. The freshness of the colours, particularly the famous 'Pompeian

156   *ISLE OF CAPRI: MARINA PICCOLA (Ch. 9) – ABOVE*
PALACE OF CASERTA: CLASSICAL FOUNTAIN (Ch. 11) – BELOW

red', is quite astonishing. On the other hand one would clearly expect to find many fine examples of the famous Roman mosaics. One celebrated example in Pompeii depicts a snarling dog with the inscription 'Cave Canem' — 'Beware the Dog'.

In both cities some of the exhibits are inevitably poignant and some positively gruesome. Plaster casts, for instance, were made of bodies where they were found overwhelmed by debris or fumes. There is even a cast of a dog clearly suffering agonised paroxysms as it slowly suffocated. At Herculaneum quite recently the remains of a boat were found containing skeletons of people clearly attempting to escape by sea.

The local guide took a gleeful delight in drawing our attention to the notorious examples of Roman pornography. These proved to be really quite small beer to people familiar with the daily dose supplied by the modern tabloid newspapers. However, one Italian matron with some small children near to us was sufficiently startled by a representation of Priapus, the god of fertility, to cry out 'Mamma mia!' and cross herself vigorously.

An interesting feature in many houses which, to be fair, the guide also pointed out specifically, was the 'larium', or household shrine with small statues of many gods, at which the master of the house would make daily offerings. This evidence of the continuing vitality of religion in the home has caused historians to revise their previous opinion that the Romans by the early Empire had relegated religion to the status of myth and legend. In a small upper room in a house in Herculaneum, thought to be probably the room of a slave, is a small cross on a wall above an altar. This, it has been claimed, may well be the earliest non-scriptural evidence of the existence of Christianity in the Roman world.

There is a fairly stiff admission charge to both sites, but once again (full marks to the Italian authorities), no charge for pensioners on production of a passport. For anyone with only time or money for one of the two, it was our fairly strong feeling that the lesser-known Herculaneum is the better bet.

So on to the villain of the piece, the volcano, Vesuvius. We were pleasantly surprised to find that Saga Holidays had no hesitation in conducting their party of veterans up the mountain itself. We had really no reason to be surprised; Saga have never treated their clientele as feeble geriatrics, and only the previous year they had unhesitatingly taken us in the opposite direction, down a salt mine in Poland. (Not on the agenda of this book unfortunately, but nevertheless one of our all-time most memorable experiences.)

Admittedly, the coach took us three-quarters of the way, but we still had about half an hour's climb to the summit on foot. Some guide books still talk of a chair-lift, but this was destroyed by an earthquake which did much damage in this part of Italy in 1980, and has not been replaced. The more nervous members of our party, not surprisingly with the evidence of Pompeii and Herculaneum fresh in our minds, had some slight misgivings. However, our excellent guide informed us that the expert vulcanologists in the observatory on the mountain had stated quite categorically 'Vesuvius will definitely not erupt today!' To which one member of the party unhelpfully replied, 'And the Met men said there definitely would not be a hurricane in England last October!'

Rosemary and I hesitated, I have to confess. Though both reasonably active septuagenarians, mountain climbing had not been on our programme of events for many years. We had indeed startled our families and friends by climbing Skiddaw and Helvellyn on our honeymoon, but that was rather a long time ago! Rosemary, as always, proposed the sensible solution. 'Let's give it a try', she said, 'but not be too proud to turn back if we are finding it too difficult'. So we decided to press on.

The path of ashes and cinders gave a surprisingly firm foothold, and the gradient was never prohibitive. The landscape, which we naturally found it prudent to pause and contemplate from time to time, was desperately dark and desolate, dominated by black lava from the last great eruption in 1944. We arrived triumphantly at the summit rather earlier than we had expected, and there we found a barrier and a charge (no concessions for pensioners!) of 3,000 lire.

Most of the guide books assert that access to the crater is permitted only with a guide. This proved to be nonsense. Apart from a vague warning to keep clear of the edge, we were left to wander around at will, completely unescorted. We gazed down, incredulous and awe-stricken into the huge, grim, yawning abyss 600 metres across and 200 metres in depth. If we had expected to find a sea of bubbling, red-hot molten lava, we would have been disappointed. A few wisps of steam were the only clues to the volcano's lethal potential.

A slightly ludicrous anti-climax was provided at the summit by a small kiosk selling postcards and souvenirs, in the charge of a frail-looking old lady. How she managed her journey to work each morning was a complete mystery. She insisted on stamping our postcards with a special logo to certify that we had genuinely vanquished Vesuvius. The descent was happily uneventful, and we settled into our seats in the coach with a quite unwarranted sense of achievement, and a feeling that Vesuvius had been in more ways than one the high spot of our tour.

Though perhaps not, at least as far as Rosemary was concerned. We discovered that there was yet another optional excursion from Paestum, this time to the famous Bénédictine Monastery of Monte Cassino. Rosemary had made a special study of medieval monasticism, so Monte Cassino, probably the most revered abbey in Christendom, mother-house of the worldwide Bénédictine Order, and the burial place of St Benedict himself, was for her an absolute must.

I remembered how on a tour of Burgundy some years earlier Rosemary had been very saddened to see the somewhat pathetic remains of the Abbey of Cluny, that other great Bénédictine Abbey, which rivalled Monte Cassino in importance and influence in the Middle Ages, and which had actually posssessed the largest church in Christendom. Cluny suffered a somewhat lingering decline. It was badly battered during the religious wars of the sixteenth century and then devastated in the upheavals following on the French Revolution. Monte Cassino, on the other hand, was utterly demolished in one fell swoop by 500 tons of American bombs on 15 February 1944.

It has been claimed that 'no event of the Second World War caused more heated and lingering controversy than the bombing of the Abbey of Monte Cassino'. At the time of the attack the abbey had been evacuated on the order of the German High Command, and its priceless manuscripts and works of art transported in lorry loads to the Vatican in Rome. Only the 80-year-old abbot, a few monks and a deaf and dumb servant remained, plus some civilian refugees from nearby villages.

As our coach slowly climbed the mountain along five miles of hairpin bends, it was easy to appreciate the great strategic significance of Monte Cassino. One writer has compared it to the Rock of Gibraltar as it commands the 'straits' at the entrance to the Liri Valley and the road to Rome. On the summit of the mountain, 1,700 feet above the valley, there now stands, gleaming in the bright Italian sunshine, the vast cream-coloured buildings of the modern monastery.

The abbey has been completely re-created on its ancient foundations almost exactly as it was before. It was reconsecrated by Pope Paul VI just 20 years after its dramatic demolition. In his homily on that occasion the Pope said, 'We should like here to pronounce the epilogue of the War — please God, of all wars. Here in forgiveness we should like to establish the brotherhood of men, to wed liberty and love to Christian peace.'

The visit to the abbey was a moving and inspiring experience. Over the main door of the abbey church, in large letters, is the single word 'PAX'. Indeed the theme of peace and reconciliation seems to permeate the entire building. One senses this immediately in the entrance cloister where a striking group of statuary depicts the dying St Benedict in the arms of his disciples. This fine modern work was presented to Monte Cassino by Chancellor Adenauer of Germany.

From there we entered the hugely impressive central cloister known as the Bramantesque, because it is in the style of that famous architect of St Peter's in Rome. At the foot of the great staircase that climbs to the door of the abbey church are statues of St Benedict and his sister, St Scholastica. This statue of St Benedict was one of the few works of art to survive the bombardment. From the top of the stairs we had a tremendous view over the valley of the River Liri. In the foreground is a monument to the Polish soldiers who were largely responsible for the final capture of Monte Cassino, of whom over 1,100 are buried in a cemetery lower down the mountain.

As we entered the church out of the dazzling Italian sunshine, we seemed at first to be in total darkness. Gradually however, as our eyes adjusted, there emerged from the gloom a marvellously ornate interior of gold, frescoes, stuccoes and polychrome marble. Incorporated wherever possible, were any fragments of the earlier abbey that could be identified. The whole church has been restored to the magnificence of the seventeenth century building that disappeared in the bombardment.

Beneath the high altar is a large crypt that contains the tombs of Saints Benedict and Scholastica, whose remains miraculously survived the devastation. Their richly ornate tomb is surrounded by a brass rail on which stand 13 lamps, dedicated as 'a symbol of faith and peace for the nations that were fighting each other in the War'.

There was an unexpected postscript to our visit to the Abbey of Monte Cassino. Shortly after our return, I wrote an article on our visit for the Catholic newspaper, *The Universe*. I was dismayed the next week to read a 'Letter to the Editor' from a gentleman who had clearly taken grave exception to what I had written. 'I am getting tired,' he wrote, 'of comments made by people such as Joseph Smith where he said that the Allies bombed the Abbey with only a handful of monks and a deaf and dumb servant inside. One suspects that Mr Smith was not there at the time . . . I can tell him that men of all religions raised a cheer when the Allied flags finally flew from the ruins of the Abbey'.

After some hesitation, because I was not keen to get involved in a public debate, I replied that I could well understand and sympathise with the strong feelings of one who was caught up in what was acknowledged to be one of the bloodiest and most savage campaigns of the war. I then went on to break to him gently that my facts were indisputably historically correct, and that even the American General Mark Clark, the Allied Supreme Commander, had admitted in his memoirs that 'the bombing of the Abbey was a tactical military mistake of the first magnitude'.

There were a few hours to spare after our visit to Monte Cassino, and Saga had neatly arranged for us to combine the abbey with the nearby Royal Palace of Caserta. If the abbey of Monte Cassino is one of the noblest houses ever erected to the greater glory of God, the Royal Palace of Caserta must be an outstanding example of man's vanity and extravagance. 'La Reggia', as it is known, was erected in the mid-eighteenth century by the Bourbon King of Naples, who desired a palace to rival that of Versailles. Most reminiscent of Versailles is the majestic park which stretches for all of three kilometres beyond the palace, adorned with a succession of classical ornamental fountains culminating in a colossal cascade and an 'English' garden.

The palace is reputed to contain 1,200 rooms, but we were escorted round a mere 12 of them by quite the most eccentric guide we have ever encountered. I think I may have hinted in earlier chapters that it has been our lot frequently on our travels to encounter some very strange and often fairly useless local guides. This chap at the Palace of Caserta was in a class of his own. He greeted us with the extraordinary introduction, 'I have to make ze apologies; I have lost my front teeth!' He then marshalled us smartly like a sergeant major and marched us into the first room. Having rattled off in a voice of Stentor a string of statistics about every *objet d'art* in the room, he then stopped abruptly and said 'Hello, next room'. This happened 12 times, when he mercifully suspended the drill and announced that we had completed the tour. He finally positioned himself strategically at the exit to the last room, and shouted in the same voice of Stentor, 'And now ladies and gentlemens, I take ze monies in all ze languages'. As the first victim dropped his contribution into his cap, he exclaimed ecstatically, 'Good, now I get rich!' Quite the most remarkable member of his profession that we had ever come across!

Back at Paestum we found there was another link with those dreadful days of 1943-4 of which we had been so powerfully reminded at Monte Cassino. When we felt like a change from wandering around the temples in that sylvan and fragrant 'zona archeologica', we would walk the mile or so down to the shore where the sand shelves gently into the Mediterranean. There is a small village, and a few bars and souvenir shops. In September it was largely deserted, though apparently in the high season Italian families with crowds of children descend upon it.

Down by the beach we found a brand new monument which told us that Paestum had also played a significant role in the history of modern times. A modest four-sided stone column bears an inscription in English and Italian:

> 'This monument was erected in humble tribute to the men of the 36th Infantry Division United States of America who lost their lives in the liberation of Italy beginning on these beaches, September 9th, 1943.'

The monument is set in a small garden. The Italian flag flies above, flanked by the Stars and Stripes on one side and the Union Jack on the other. From the beaches the action apparently moved immediately north, and the ancient Greek temples, little more than a mile from the landings, exactly like Bayeux and the tapestry in Normandy, miraculously escaped unharmed. The ancient Greeks would certainly have considered that Poseidon, the god of the sea, who had preserved Poseidonia through the vicissitudes of all those centuries, was again taking good care of his own.

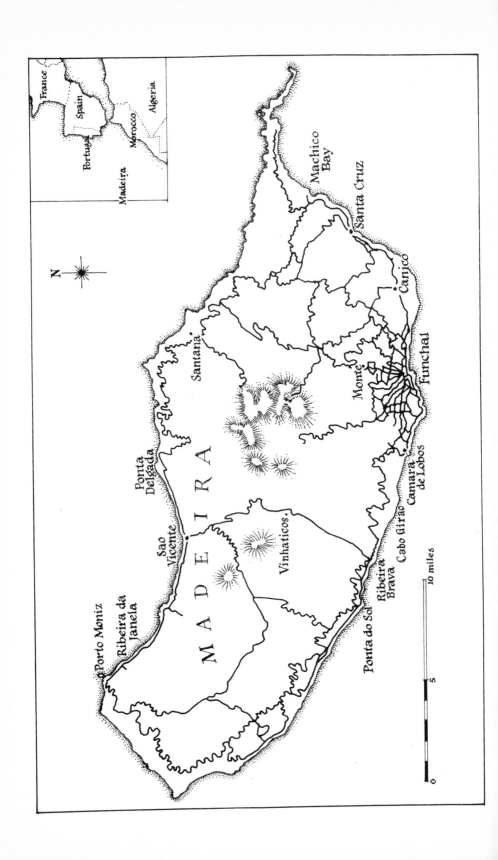

CHAPTER TEN

Madeira

We travelled to Madeira in October 1989 at rather short notice. We had been compelled to cancel a planned tour of Turkey in September because my wife had been taken suddenly ill. This presented several problems since I also had a commission to write about the Turkey trip for *The Observer* newspaper. However, Frances Liddiard, the public relations executive of Saga who had masterminded our previous trips, came up with the very kind suggestion that we could be transferred to a holiday in Madeira later in October. This would be less strenuous and a suitable convalescence for Rosemary. Desmond Balmer, the travel editor of *The Observer*, showed equal kindness and consideration by readily switching his commission from Turkey to Madeira.

When the transfer was first mooted, I had to think very hard to remember where Madeira was! All that Rosemary could recall was that the famous Duke of Clarence had drowned in a butt of malmsey, the island's best-known product. A glance at the map reminded us that Madeira was an island in the Atlantic on approximately the same line of latitude as Casablanca in North Africa. Perusal of the publicity material was certainly encouraging: 'Europe's Tropical Garden with 2,000 different species of flora, an ideal climate and a breathtaking splendour and variety of landscapes.' We had long since learned, of course, to take travel brochures with a pinch of salt, but in this case when we reached Madeira the reality genuinely matched the publicity.

We next realised that there was a direct link with that excellent holiday that we had enjoyed in Portugal. There we had been fascinated by the story of the 'Age of Discoveries' and Prince Henry the Navigator's school at Sagres near 'The End of the World'. Madeira, we learned, was one of the first of those discoveries, when his captains Zarco and Teixeira landed at what is now known as Machico Bay in 1419.

Our hotel, the five-star Atlantis, stood high above that Bay of Machico with magnificent views all around. All the hotels in which we have been housed on our Saga tours have generally been luxurious in both their furnishings and their catering, but none, I think, has quite equalled the Atlantis. Other members of the party were accommodated at the Dom Pedro Hotel on the edge of the village of Machico, and were equally enthusiastic about their hotel.

The elegance of the spacious corridors and lounges of the Atlantis was enhanced by glorious arrangements of one of the island's many floral specialities, the strelizia or bird of paradise flower. These spectacular flowers, which really do look like colourful tropical birds in flight, appear to be as versatile and long-lasting as they are beautiful. We found them later making magnificent displays out of doors, but equally adorning the statues and altars inside the many churches and shrines of the island.

As for food, we were astonished on our first morning to be confronted with a most remarkable buffet breakfast. As seasoned travellers around Europe, we are familiar and reasonably happy with the typical 'continental' breakfast of coffee, bread and jam. At the Atlantis there was choice from unlimited supplies of fried egg and bacon, sausage, cheese, cold meats and cereals, tea, coffee and fruit juices. If you fancied a boiled egg, you could choose from those boiled for 'five minutos' or seven. Other meals were on the same scale. At dinner there were always two 'starters' rather than one, and a wide choice of main courses to follow.

But of course we hadn't come to Madeira for the food, but for the climate, the scenery and the flowers. We had a fairly sensational introduction to the island's incredible floral riches by a visit on our first full day to the Jardim Botanico in Funchal, the capital of Madeira. Here I shall have to be careful to temper my enthusiasm and moderate my superlatives, because I suspect that I may already have risked boring the reader with my panegyrics about the gardens of Giverny, Ravello and Andalucia.

Where the Jardim Botanico scores over even those famous gardens is in the sheer variety of the exotic fruit and flowers made possible by the island's remarkable climate. The temperature rarely falls below 60°F in winter or rises above 75°F in the height of summer. Not only in the Jardim Botanico, but everywhere in Madeira, we found orange groves, banana plants in huge quantities, jacarandas, outdoor poinsettias, eucalyptus trees, paw-paws and passion fruit, plus arthuriums shaped like bright red arum lilies, as well as the hibiscus, oleanders and bougainvillaea with which we were already familiar in many parts of the Mediterranean region.

I am also uncomfortably conscious of the fact that in earlier chapters I have been less than charitable in my strictures on the shortcomings of many local guides that we have had to suffer. In the Jardim Botanico at Funchal we first met Grace who was to accompany us on most of our later excursions. Grace was a paragon amongst guides. We warmed to her immediately because of the brief but informative commentaries she fluently provided on the various items of botanical interest, all in perfectly idiomatic and grammatical English with scarcely a trace of a foreign accent.

She could be wittily amusing as well as helpfully informative. For instance, she gave us some useful advice on the island's special drinks. Madeira had much to offer in this regard, she insisted, quite apart from the famous malmsey. There was the soft drink 'maracuja' or passion fruit juice, which was an excellent thirst quencher. She also strongly recommended another Madeiran speciality 'poncha', a sort of cocktail made of rum, honey and orange juice. Visitors, she said, always found a 'poncha' most agreeable, and two even better, while after three, they began to speak fluent Portuguese.

I had presumed that Grace, a young girl in her twenties, must have spent some time in England, probably studying English at university. I took an opportunity to congratulate her on her splendid English and to enquire where she had learned it. Unbelievably she replied that she had never been outside Madeira, and had learned her English at school and later at evening classes. This was a sobering thought indeed for a one-time educationist, who, like so many others, had struggled with the notorious inability of the English to master foreign languages. The usual excuse is that we are an island race who over the centuries have been insulated from the foreigner across the Channel. England is an island some 20 miles from the mainland of Europe; Madeira is 550 miles away.

We moved on into the centre of Funchal, which is immediately recognisable as Portuguese, indeed almost a miniature Lisbon, with streets similarly sloping down to the harbour where great cruise liners can often be seen. Even the pavements are attractively decorated in similar black and white mosaics as in Lisbon. In a prominent position in the centre of the city we noticed an impressive statue, which, from a distance, we presumed would be our old friend Prince Henry the Navigator. However, it turned out to be another famous explorer, Christopher Columbus no less, who lived in Funchal at one time.

The cathedral of Funchal is a relatively small building in the Portuguese Manueline style, with a plain white exterior but lots of baroque ornamentation inside. The interior was disappointingly dark, which effectively prevented us from fully appreciating the many fine works of art that the guide books had led us to expect. On the other hand, this was perhaps the only cathedral of the scores that we have visited all over Europe, where the locals, quietly saying their prayers, far outnumbered the tourists wandering round the building.

We found more evidence of the piety and religious fervour of the islanders when we attended Sunday Mass in Machico. We arrived early before the previous Mass had finished, and were astonished to find this quite sizeable church packed to the doors with an overflow of hundreds of worshippers on their knees in the square outside. It was the same again at the next Mass. Only in Poland have we observed scenes comparable to these.

Not far from the church in Machico is a chapel known locally as 'The Chapel of the Miracles'. There is a romantic legend that when Zarco and Teixeira, Prince Henry's captains, landed at Machico, they found the grave of two English lovers who had been shipwrecked on the then uninhabited island almost a century before, when fleeing the wrath of their parents. They are supposed to have been buried by their surviving companions, who then managed to sail away. Teixeira, who became governor of this area of the island, lent credence to the legend by building a chapel on the site of the grave. This 'Chapel of the Miracles' was later destroyed by floods in

1803, but the original doorway survives. Above the altar is a much venerated cedar cross which was rescued from the sea after the flood, and is claimed to be the original cross which stood above the grave of the legendary lovers. The simple beauty of the interior of the chapel is again wonderfully enhanced by striking arrangements of the bird of paradise flowers.

I mentioned earlier the remarkably high standards of both the quality and quantity of the catering on the island. Fish naturally features prominently on the menus, and one has the comforting knowledge that it comes not from the heavily polluted Mediterranean, but from the pure, icy depths of the Atlantic Ocean. This applies particularly to an almost unique Madeiran speciality, the 'espada', correctly translated not as swordfish, but the black scabbard fish.

These strange creatures, found only off the coasts of Madeira and some parts of Japan, exist at great depths on the bed of the ocean. They can be caught only at night by vessels equipped with special tackle and bright lights which lure the fish up a few thousand feet. When landed on deck they are dead and bloodless through compression, jet black with great bulging eyes, and absolutely hideous to look at, but they make an extremely tasty dish.

We also found that 'espada' was delicious in sandwiches as a midday snack. However, as always on Madeira, if you asked for one, you got two. Rosemary and I thought we would try more Madeiran products, an orange for her and a banana for me. We were served with two of each, with the oranges and bananas both neatly peeled and quartered. In case you are suspecting that all this may have been due to language difficulties, this was certainly not so; everybody everywhere that we came into contact with in shops, hotels, restaurants etc. had workable English.

Madeira is rightly renowned for its excellent weather and remarkably equable climate all the year round. There are occasional exceptions, however, as we certainly discovered when literally out of the blue an Atlantic storm of unbelievable ferocity suddenly struck the island. The wind howled and screamed incessantly, making such a din that we could scarcely hear ourselves speak in our eighth-floor room. We retreated therefore to the lounges on the ground floor while the rain bucketed down non-stop and the temperature plummeted. Then, almost as abruptly as after the storm in Beethoven's 'Pastoral Symphony', the scene changed, and we awoke next morning to another hot summer's day in late October.

However, the wasted day was greatly improved by an astonishing encounter with a fellow resident. The hotel provided tea and biscuits each day at four o'clock for anybody interested, so, while the storm raged, we took advantage of this. An old lady of 85 travelling alone, and as bright as a button, invited us to join her. Her only noticeable idiosyncrasy was that she tended to address the waiters in Portuguese, although, of course, they understood English perfectly well. In conversation at the tea-table we discovered to our amazement that our paths had crossed over 50 years previously, when she had been a lecturer in modern languages at the university where we were students. We spent a delightful half-hour reminiscing about mutual acquaintances from those days, and, I regret to say, exchanging a few scurrilous anecdotes!

This delightful encounter was really not surprising, because in the earlier chapter on Portugal I described how one of the great advantages of Saga holidays is the rare quality of the company. It was certainly the same again in Madeira. In addition to the wonderful old girl just mentioned, with whom we had more rewarding conversations, we dined most evenings with Ken and Betty, who had both come safely through major crises in their lives, but were now enjoying their retirement with commendable serenity. Ken had spent most of the war as a prisoner of the Japanese, but was able to look back on that ghastly experience philosophically and without rancour. Betty had won her battle against a more insidious personal threat, cancer. They were both most agreeable and stimulating company at the Atlantis dinner-table.

We naturally took full advantage of various coach tours to see as much as possible of this wonderfully scenic island. As we passed by the endless succession of banana plantations, the invaluable Grace explained the method of cultivation. Each plant produces only one bunch of bananas, although this can weigh anything up to 40 kilos. The bananas are cut when still green but just beginning to turn yellow. The plant is then uprooted and replaced by one of its off-shoots (one of its 'babies' in Grace's charming phrase). These Madeiran bananas are rather smaller and slightly sweeter than the West Indian variety, and are almost all exported to Portugal.

We stopped at Monte, a suburb high in the hills above Funchal, with a fine baroque church which contains the tomb of the last Emperor of Austria who lived in exile in Madeira after the First World War. However, the place is better known as the starting point of a strange traditional entertainment, a toboggan run down the bumpy hillside. Tourists can hurtle down the slopes in sledges controlled by men in white slacks and straw hats. Apparently this bizarre entertainment has been a family business for generations. We were not tempted to join in what has clearly become a tourist gimmick. A friend of mine who was on a cruise which included Madeira in its itinerary, told me that the ship stayed in Funchal harbour just long enough for the passengers to try the toboggan run and drink a glass of malmsey, and nothing else.

A tour of the dramatic coastal scenery of Madeira was certainly exciting, if not positively unnerving. We first passed through the picturesque fishing village of Camara de Lobos. The exquisite beauty of this place brought Winston Churchill here on a painting holiday when out of office in 1950. Then on to Cabo Girao, which claims the highest sea cliff in Europe and the second highest in the world. Some stretches of this tour, along narrow roads round tortuous hairpin bends with sheer cliff faces immediately below, reminded us irresistibly of the celebrated Amalfi Drive in southern Italy described in the last chapter. The Madeiran coach driver, however, did not have the benefit of expert Italian road and bridge engineering to help him along this breathtaking corniche road. The comparison with the Amalfi Drive even extended to the vegetable plots cultivated in terraces at most improbable angles down the cliff sides. We have rarely contributed the routine tip to the driver more readily when he brought us safely back to base.

Grace, who had evidently noticed the nervous looks of some of the passengers, filled in a small delay in the proceedings with a little story. A coach driver from Madeira and a priest both died on the same day, and arrived together at the Pearly Gates. However, St

Peter told them that unfortunately there was only one vacancy, so that one of them would have to find accommodation elsewhere. The coach driver was naturally despondent; being used to the ideal climate of Madeira, he did not fancy the other place at all. He presumed that the reverend who had spent all his life praying and preaching would surely be given priority. To his great delight, however, it was he, the coach driver, that St Peter beckoned to come forward. 'You see,' said St Peter, 'when the clergyman was preaching, the congregation was usually asleep; but when you were driving your coach, the passengers were all praying like mad!'

The mountainous interior of Madeira is just as scenically spectacular as that dramatic road round the edge of the island. From a succession of belvederes affording stunning views, we remember particularly those above the so-called 'crater village'. This remarkable village, till quite recently completely isolated, nestles at the foot of a cirque of spectacular extinct volcanoes. Michelin, in a rare poetic passage, says 'The white houses of the village lie scattered like stars around a hollow circle of ravine-scarred mountains'. There is nowadays a steep, tortuous road which connects the village with the outside world. The whole area has a quite exceptional and highly photogenic beauty.

As I have mentioned before, an evening of folk music is frequently a pleasant feature of Saga holidays. The Madeiran version was one of the best ever, and bore a distinct family likeness to the one that we had enjoyed in Portugal. The entertainment was provided, as in Portugal, by a group of very youthful singers and dancers from Machico, who performed *fortissimo* with great energy and infectious enthusiasm. One interesting difference from the Portuguese evening was that the singing and dancing was accompanied on some unusual, traditional Madeiran musical instruments.

Another difference was typical of Madeira; the entertainment was accompanied by a meal of 'espada', tuna or chicken, preceded by a glass of malmsey and washed down with more Madeiran wine or passion fruit juice. Again as in Portugal, this hugely enjoyable entertainment concluded with an invitation to the audience to join in. This time there was no escape. Encouraged by the Saga staff, and led by the singers and dancers, we all formed into one enormous

conga, which circled right round the restaurant.

Our experience of Madeira had more than justified that brochure blurb about 'Europe's Tropical Garden with a breathtaking splendour and variety of landscapes'. We had just one reservation, however. Some outer areas of Funchal are a mess. A ring road and a huge bridge were under construction, and there was talk of a major extension to the airport. Hotels and luxury homes seemed to be springing up without much obvious planning control. Bulldozers, cranes and general builders' clutter mingled incongruously with the floral exotica, much as we had noticed earlier in Athens on our first Saga holiday, to Greece. Some locals were apprehensive that their lovely island was under threat from rampant tourism and developers. 'The nouveaux riches are taking over', complained Grace.

One visitor at least was untroubled by such thoughts. On our last evening in Madeira we walked up to the marvellous viewpoint above the hotel. We were joined by a complete stranger. 'I'm planning three more visits here', he said. 'I feel that I must see this wonderful island in all four seasons of the year'. We knew just how he felt.

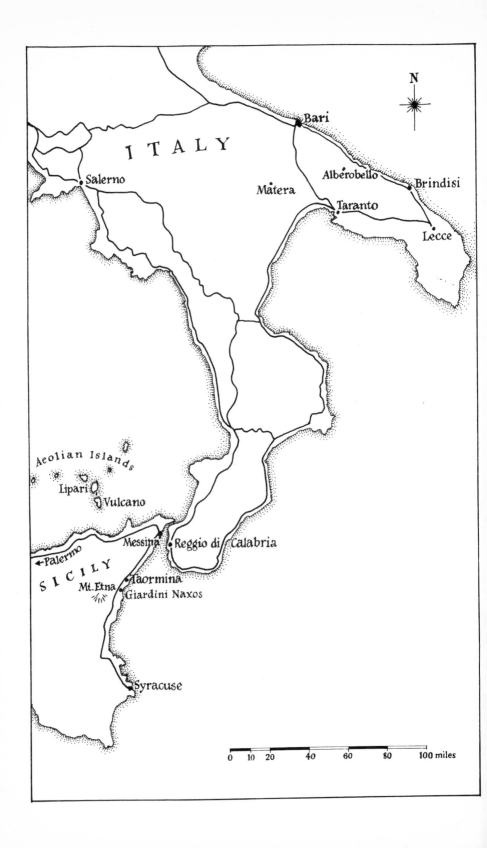

N

ITALY

Salerno

Bari

Alberobello

Brindisi

Matera

Taranto

Lecce

Aeolian Islands

Lipari

Vulcano

Messina

Reggio di Calabria

←Palermo

SICILY

Mt.Etna

Taormina

Giardini Naxos

Syracuse

0 10 20   40   60   80   100 miles

CHAPTER ELEVEN

Sicily and Southern Italy

N o sooner had I cheerfully accepted an invitation from Saga to join their holiday in Sicily and southern Italy than our TV screens were filled with frightening pictures of Mt Etna erupting and threatening to engulf half of Sicily. A few days later the Mafia perpetrated two particularly revolting murders.

The omens therefore did not seem very propitious. The possibility did just flicker across my mind that perhaps I should check with Saga that the tour was still going ahead, but I quickly dismissed the thought. Less experienced travellers might have been deterred, but not Saga's veterans. Readers of the earlier chapter on Paestum will recall that we had been unhesitatingly conducted up Vesuvius. Nor on our tour of Poland, not recorded in this book, had we boggled at the far more intimidating prospect of a descent of several thousand feet in total darkness into the bowels of a Polish salt-mine. Saga travellers would not be put off by a mere volcano, or indeed the worst that the Mafia could do.

At the beginning of this chapter I said I 'cheerfully' accepted Saga's invitation. In truth, however, there was a real element of sadness as well. In the last chapter I mentioned my wife's sudden illness, and the hope that the holiday in Madeira would prove a suitable convalescence to hasten her recovery. So for a time it did, and we even managed another Saga trip a little later to two parts of ill-fated Yugoslavia, also for obvious reasons not included in this book. Unhappily, however, it soon became apparent that her illness was progressive, and finally, albeit most reluctantly, I had to accept the fact that she needed expert full-time care in a nursing home.

At first I could not contemplate further expeditions abroad without her loving, knowledgeable and wholly supportive companionship. However, I was finally persuaded by family and friends that with the comforting certainty that she was being very well cared for in the nursing home, it would be foolish to refuse an occasional break from my daily visits. And so with commissions to write about the holiday from *The Universe* and *The Observer*, I decided, though still with some misgivings, to accept the invitation.

It was then that Eric came to the rescue. He and his wife were long-standing friends of Rosemary and myself with similar interests in travel abroad. We had even assisted each other in planning holidays in the past, and usually exchanged notes and pictures afterwards. When Eric most kindly volunteered to accompany me, my doubts disappeared. The Saga party in due course had reason to be grateful to me for bringing him along. Eric is an artist, and brought all his working clobber with him. He soon became the celebrity of the party; people watched fascinated as he rapidly transferred to paper the sights and scenes of our travels. Commissions for pictures as souvenirs rapidly flowed in.

Our first introduction to Sicily was certainly encouraging. We were based for four nights in the pleasant little seaside town of Giardini Naxos. If Il Tritone, our small family-run hotel, lacked the magnificence of the Atlantis in Madeira, it made up for it in the warm and friendly attentiveness of the staff, and particularly Maria, the English wife of the proprietor. This pleasant small hotel was situated on the coast road that ran right round a picturesque bay. From the balcony of our room we looked straight out on to the ever-blue Mediterranean only a few yards across the road.

We had no time at all to worry about Etna. On the first morning we set off by coach for an exploration of that enormous volcano. It quickly became apparent that Etna is a very different proposition indeed from Vesuvius. Etna is a vast smouldering massif, Vesuvius a mere peak.

As the coach slowly climbed from the coast, the driver was soon in difficulties as he negotiated the endless tricky hairpin bends with an engine that tended to overheat. The scenery became steadily more barren and forbidding, until it finally degenerated into a wilderness of black solidified lava. Particularly fascinating was the river of lava from that latest eruption which had looked so terrifying on our television screens. Total disaster, we were told, had been narrowly averted; the stream of lava had already devoured two houses on the edge of a village when the frantic efforts of engineers and vulcanologists halted it just in the nick of time.

The coach parked at around 6,000 feet. There are always some tough and adventurous members of a Saga party who are game for anything. These decided to venture a further 2,000 feet up the mountain via an expensive and dodgy-looking cable car. At the other end of the party spectrum, the least energetic were content to stroll around in the sunshine admiring the fantastic scenery. The majority, including Eric and me, opted for a short but strenuous climb to a new mini-crater, christened San Silvestri, the latest of the many small craters that pop up regularly on the surface of this vast volcano.

The route lay along a trail of ash and cinders, extremely reminiscent of the last lap to the summit of Vesuvius, and presented a reasonably firm foothold that caused no problems even for veterans like us. When we arrived at the mini-crater, some people were mildly disappointed to find no smoke or glowing lava, but others were rather startled to realise that the ground beneath our feet was distinctly warm. During most of the morning there had been clouds obscuring the summit, but just as we reached our mini-crater these clouds miraculously lifted, and we were rewarded with staggering views over the whole of that gigantic, lunar landscape right up to the topmost tip of the mountain. And, of course, cameras were busily snapping, and Eric was hard at work with his sketch pad.

When we descended from San Silvestri, we naturally were ready for some relaxation in a nearby bar. The proprietor evidently felt that his unusually elderly customers were in need of restoratives, and insisted on presenting us each with a complimentary glass of the local liqueur, appropriately named 'Fire of Etna'. It was the most lethal liquid we had ever sampled, and quite undrinkable. 'Gosh,' said one startled pensioner, 'it must be paint-stripper!' I'm afraid nobody bought any.

The Sicilians, we were told, while always conscious of the potential perils of their volcano, nevertheless generally regard Etna as a friend and benefactor. Most of the roads on the island are paved with blocks of lava, for instance, and lava is the commonest building material. At the lower reaches of the mountain, lava from earlier eruptions gradually breaks down into highly fertile soil. On this base a wide range of Mediterranean fruit, vegetables and even vines happily flourish. All these crops, presumably, have the unusual advantage of free, in-built under-soil heating.

All this interesting information was supplied to us by Terry, our exceptionally able and ever-helpful Saga courier, who later in the holiday went to extraordinary lengths to ensure that some unexpected problems were satisfactorily resolved. Unlike some of our local guides, whom I have regarded with modified rapture in earlier chapters, Saga's representatives on these holidays have always been of a uniformly high standard.

I remember especially two Saga couriers from countries for various reasons not represented in this book. Andrew in Poland was an able young man who had spent some time as a student in England, and was able to compare for us most interestingly the respective educational systems. The aspect of the communist education system in Poland that struck us most forcibly was that it was totally free at every stage from nursery school to university. Whether this happy state of affairs still continues, I rather doubt. Andrew was also most enlightening on the reasonably successful cohabitation of communism and Catholicism in Poland. The greatest failure of the communist system as he saw it (when he had carefully checked that there was no possibility of being overheard), was the chronic shortage of affordable housing; it was commonplace, he said, for young couples to have to move in with their parents for up to 15 years till they could get a home of their own.

We also look back with gratitude and affection to Jadran, the Saga courier on the Island of Krk, in what used to be the popular holiday country of Yugoslavia. We have often wondered how he will have fared in the present troubles; at best he will certainly have lost his job. Ironically and tragically, Jadran was brimming with enthusiasm for the new devolved government of Croatia under the first-ever elected President Franjo Tudjman. Everyone was pulling together impressively, said Jadran; the chronic Yugoslav inflation had been virtually eliminated, and a rosy future lay ahead. Looking back it seems to us absolutely criminal that fallacious and outdated notions of extreme nationalism should have brought that beautiful country to its present sorry state.

Nor must I forget Kathy at Paestum who had been brought in from Spain at short notice in an emergency, but who, in a sort of personal Ibero-Italian which caused much mutual hilarity, ensured with a quiet determination that our interests were entirely protected. In only one small detail were her efforts comparatively unavailing. The hotel had apparently not been familiar with the Saga tradition of a final farewell celebration dinner, but the chef had clearly set out to do his best on this occasion. So for the main course each guest was solemnly presented with an enormous plate of 'frutta di mare', an astonishing assortment of leathery squid and shiny, spiny shellfish of every conceivable variety. One lady with whom we had become very friendly, took one appalled look at her plate, turned pale and fled from the room.

However, let us return to Sicily, since the last few paragraphs have been merely a preamble to stating quite unequivocally that Teresa ('Terry' for short) was easily the Queen of Saga representatives. She never hesitated in her masterly Italian to protect her clients against the occasional shortcomings of coach drivers, barmen, guides, restaurateurs or anyone else with whom we came into contact. Her *pièce de résistance* (or whatever that is in Italian), came when the tourists at the back of our coach began to complain of poisonous fumes penetrating into the coach from its exhaust. With steely insistence she bullied the reluctant driver into telephoning his HQ, and demanding that a replacement coach be instantly despatched. It meant a wasted couple of hours, but the sufferers in the rear were mightily relieved.

Sicily has some more interesting volcanic activity to show in the shape of the Aeolian islands off its north coast. These islands, Lipari, Stromboli and Vulcano, were named after Aeolus, the ancient Greek god of the winds, who imprisoned his charges here. He let them loose, according to Homer and Virgil, with devastating effect upon both Odysseus and Aeneas on their travels. More recently, Mussolini found the islands a convenient prison in which to incarcerate his political enemies.

We first visited Lipari, the largest of the three, long regarded as an extinct volcano, and, in fact, now rapidly growing in popularity as a holiday resort, particularly with Germans. Lipari can offer some delightful coastal scenery for the delectation of its visitors, but with just one blot on the landscape — an enormous white gash on one hillside marks the area from which is quarried Europe's main supply of pumice stone.

We moved on to the next island, Vulcano, which, of course, gave its name to all subsequent exploding mountains. Vulcano is certainly one of the weirdest places that we have ever visited. As our boat entered the harbour, we were greeted by a rather offensive, acrid smell. The stink got steadily worse after we had disembarked and walked towards a large pool of hot, sulphurous mud in which bathers, particularly Germans, were eagerly wallowing up to their necks. Some had even plastered their faces with the stuff. This highly unpleasant hot bath, Terry informed us, is claimed to work wonders for sufferers from arthritis, rheumatism and similar complaints.

'Mud, mud, glorious mud', the celebrated ballad of Flanders and Swann, inevitably came to mind, 'Nothing quite like it for cooling the blood'. But definitely not this mud! When the bathers can't stand the heat or the smell any longer, they clamber over the rocks and slide down into the sea to clean themselves up. They can't stay there long either, because the seawater is also unpleasantly hot and even dangerously radioactive. A little further along there is a more normal sort of beach, except that the sand is nearly black, while the whole area is surrounded by rocks of various fantastic shapes in a mixture of shades of red, yellow and orange.

Most of our party were more than content just to be spectators of this bizarre scene, while Eric, of course, was busy sketching the weird and colourful rock configurations that were all around. However, one indomitable and presumably arthritic old girl, clearly determined not to miss out on this unique therapeutic opportunity, whipped off her frock and plunged into the mud up to her neck in her undies. And thence in this unconventional garb into the sea.

Vulcano last erupted in 1890 and is now reckoned to be totally extinct and no longer a menace. We were puzzled, therefore, to see plumes of white smoke seeping from various points around the summit. Presumably these must be of no great significance in the opinion of the expert vulcanologists. Nevertheless, one couldn't help wondering whether Vulcano might still be capable of one final, farewell performance. After all, the Romans were quite certain that Vesuvius was extinct in AD 79.

All this remarkable volcanic activity in and around Sicily we found absolutely fascinating. However, I had expected the main interest of Sicily for me to be the extensive remains from the period of the occupation of the island by the Greeks. These, I knew, included some of the finest to have survived from the greatest period of the ancient Greek civilisation. In the chapter on Paestum I wrote at some length about the extraordinary readiness of the Greeks to establish colonies, which were simply new Greek cities, all around the Mediterranean area. The greatest concentration of these colonies, and some of the finest examples, are in the 'Magna Graecia' area of southern Italy in general, but above all in Sicily.

The first, and one of the finest examples we visited, was at Taormina at the end of our tour of the area dominated by Mount Etna. This picturesque little town, which stands high on a terrace overlooking the sea, is claimed by many to be the most beautiful spot in the whole of Sicily. It possesses a notable theatre built by the Greeks in the third century BC but later re-modelled and extended by the Romans, as is clear from the prominent amount of the familiar Roman brickwork.

Like so many ancient Greek theatres, this example at Taormina is remarkable for its excellent acoustics. It has also the unique advantage of the majestic and usually snow-covered cone of Mt Etna as a dramatic backcloth to the auditorium. This fine theatre is still in use, and every summer there is a festival of classical plays. Unfortunately from our point of view, scenery in process of erection for the current production prevented our enjoyment of the celebrated vista of Mt Etna.

There are similar examples of the Greek colonisation of Sicily to be seen all over the island. The finest examples are naturally in Syracuse, which grew and prospered so remarkably after its foundation by the Corinthians in 734 BC that it eventually ruled the whole of Sicily and rivalled even Athens as the greatest city of the ancient Greek world. The local guide in Syracuse chose to start the tour with a visit to the substantial remains of the Roman temple of Diana. 'Not your Diana', he said in an irreverent aside. We next visited the cathedral, which is a quite extraordinary mixture of architectural styles. The building was erected on the site of a Greek temple of the fifth century BC and many of the original Greek columns were incorporated. It received other additions in various styles over the centuries, and finally an intricate Baroque façade. Our tour of the cathedral was enlivened by the unexpected appearance of a picturesque Italian wedding, with all the traditional flamboyant attire and incessant blaring of motor car horns.

Then on to the vast 'zona archeologica', where the number one attraction without any doubt is the great Greek theatre, claimed to be the largest in the Greek world as well as probably the best preserved. The theatre was built in the fifth century BC, early enough for it to present the first performance of *The Persians* by Aeschylus, which the great tragedian, himself for some years resident in Syracuse, actually attended in person. The theatre can accommodate 15,000 people, and like its smaller sister at Taormina, is still used for a spring festival of classical plays.

Another classical site, again one of the largest of its kind anywhere, is the Roman amphitheatre of the first century AD. The guide drew our attention with a certain ghoulish relish to the entrances and tunnels through which the gladiators and wild beasts would make their entry for the bloody combats which were such an unpleasant feature of the Roman world of the Augustan period and beyond.

Even more unpleasant are the associations of the nearby enormous stone quarries, latterly overgrown with colourful vegetation and even orange groves, so much so that the painter Caravaggio gave his picture of the scene the title 'Latomia del Paradiso', 'Paradise Quarry'. Paradise would be the last name that the Athenian captives would have been likely to use, when 7,000 of them were imprisoned here in savagely inhumane conditions after the total disaster of the 'Great Expedition' that Athens mounted against

Syracuse in 413 BC.

One detail of these caves or quarries which seemed particularly to intrigue many members of our party was the so-called 'Ear of Dionysius', a large ear-shaped cave hewn out of the solid rock, which is credited with the possession of a remarkable echo. Syracuse, a city of over 300,000 inhabitants during its greatest period, was ruled by a succession of more or less benevolent 'tyrants'. 'The Ear of Dionysius' gets its name because one of the most famous of these tyrants, Dionysius, was supposed to be able to employ the echo to listen in to the conversations of his enemies imprisoned in the cave — evidently a primitive form of bugging or telephone tapping!

After a week or so of pretty strenuous sightseeing, including that memorable but tiring tour of Etna, I decided that I would appreciate a day's relaxation while Eric took his pad and pencils to see what opportunities for his art were presented by the Roman villa at Casale with its famous mosaic floors. I was sunning myself on the balcony of our room which overlooked the blue Mediterranean and the main road around the lovely bay, when my attention was attracted by some peculiar proceedings on a pedestrian crossing almost immediately below. As a motorist who has clocked up many thousands of miles touring the countries of western Europe, I have tended to agree with the general opinion that Italian drivers are the worst of the lot, and certainly the least law-abiding. I have always charitably regarded their failings in this respect as the inevitable concomitant of the pleasantly happy-go-lucky, uninhibited side of their character.

The activities on that pedestrian crossing were becoming odder by the minute. I had a sudden inspiration. As a former teacher, I remembered those enterprising colleagues who used to encourage civic responsibility in their pupils by sending them out on useful local enquiries of various kinds, including traffic surveys. (Being long retired, I have no idea whether such frivolities are any longer permissible inside the strait-jacket of the National Curriculum.) However, I decided that I would attempt to study the psychology of the Italian road user. I would log the strange happenings on that pedestrian crossing below; I would do a Sicilian traffic survey!

This pedestrian crossing, clearly marked, was obviously badly needed, since the road along the promenade was a busy main thoroughfare. The first thing that struck me as strange was the sight of the proprietor of the bar next door happily setting out white plastic tables and chairs in the roadway on the pedestrian crossing, thus effectively gumming up one end, and rendering it useless for its intended purpose.

Soon a car pulled up alongside the tables and chairs, and the driver wandered into the bar. A few minutes later a second car double parked, completely blocking the crossing and the road. This driver, leaving his engine running, also sauntered into the bar. The inevitable denouement followed, of course, when a coach arrived and the driver, his way completely blocked, hooted incessantly and furiously as only an Italian can. The offending motorist, after an interval of bedlam, strolled nonchalantly out of the bar, and drove off without a word of apology.

At this point I adjourned for lunch. When I returned to my observation post, a youth on a Vespa scooter drew up on the pedestrian crossing. Whereupon a girl who had been sitting on the seawall, walked across, kissed him tenderly on both cheeks, and engaged him in animated conversation. Another girl then arrived in a car and joined them on the crossing. Next a youth from the seawall leaned across her passenger seat and contrived with some difficulty to kiss her on both cheeks. Finally a third girl arrived on a Vespa scooter and completed the total occupation of the crossing while she kissed and conversed with all previous arrivals. Once again a furious and frustrated motorist hooted non-stop until the youths and maidens slowly and reluctantly sorted themselves out and departed. During the whole of my period of observation not a single pedestrian attempted to make any use of the crossing.

In writing the foregoing I do not wish to appear to speak disparagingly of the southern Italians, who are among my favourite people. As I have said, they have many admirable qualities; they are cheerful, generous and courteous. They are passionately fond of children and produce them in large quantities. They are also a people of deep faith. We noticed that, in contrast to us indifferent or agnostic Anglo-Saxons, they throng their churches and belt out the hymns with gusto. Perhaps it is this faith which is the reason why these Vespasians scorn the use of helmets and the motorists rarely wear seat belts. However, their cavalier attitude to the internal combustion engine is incomprehensible to us cautious and generally law-abiding northerners.

Why then do the authorities bother to mark out pedestrian crossings if nobody takes the slightest notice of them, and the police invariably turn a blind eye to offenders? I put the question to the wise and knowledgeable Terry. 'Well', she said, after a moment's reflection, 'if you are fortunate enough to get killed on a pedestrian crossing, you will posthumously be eligible for greatly enhanced insurance payments'. The moral is, if you are a member of a Saga party in Italy who rather likes a post-prandial stroll, be careful not to venture on to a pedestrian crossing; it might be fatal. I sent these musings, after our return home, to the *Guardian* under the title 'Sicilian Vespas'. I thought the pun-loving *Guardian* might like that. However, some sub-editor sent the standard reply that they had too much Italian material already.

When the entertainment provided by the pantomime on the pedestrian crossing began to pall, I decided to take a stroll along the promenade until Eric and the rest of the party returned from their excursion. There something else unusual caught my attention, namely a small, rather grimy drinking fountain with white supporting panels engraved with some curious inscriptions. The first of these merely indicated its date, 1932, just one year before the first of my many visits to Italy. That was the pilgrimage to Rome as a member of a school party during Mussolini's fascist regime, which I mentioned in the Prologue to this book.

The other inscriptions on this rather uninviting fountain were in Latin and clearly confirmed its date of origin. 'Ex fascibus salus' said one, which I took to mean 'Salvation through fascism'. A second said 'Agere non loqui' — 'Deeds not words', while a third was presumably another fascist maxim, 'Memento audere semper' — 'Always remember to be bold'. However, I was amused to observe that some dissenting vandal who evidently knew his Latin, had made a clumsy, but still legible emendation to 'Memento *audire* semper' — 'Always remember to listen!' Two further inscriptions simply put the fountain's date in contemporary fascist terminology. 'Anno X E.F.' was about right, since Mussolini seized power around 1922, which would make 1932 the tenth year of the fascist regime. The last inscription really puzzled me, however. It said 'Anno 2865 di Roma', presumably meaning the 2,865th year of the existence of Rome. However, the traditional date for the foundation of ancient Rome is certainly 753 BC, which added to AD 1932 gives 2,685 and not 2,865. Whose arithmetic was wrong, mine or Mussolini's, or was it just a misprint?

The unexpected encounter with this peculiar relic of the 1930s inevitably revived memories of that first of my many visits to various parts of Italy. In 1933 Mussolini was at the height of his power. I'm afraid that we young teenagers in that school party were not sophisticated enough to sense the sinister undertones of his regime. In any case, we were still in the shadow of 1914-18 and the great 'war to end wars'. And had we not now got the League of Nations, which would certainly prevent the possibility of future conflagrations? We merely thought the fascists rather pompous and slightly ridiculous. I myself almost fell foul of the regime as soon as we entered Italy. We were travelling overnight on the train from Paris, and with youthful bravado I had settled down for sleep with my feet up on the seat opposite. I was rudely awakened by a nasty-looking chap in a black shirt shouting at me in a threatening manner. He was also brandishing a notebook, and it was obvious to me and my companions that he was proposing to fine me on the spot. Of course, we pretended that we didn't know what he was going on about, and he finally departed in disgust. I was afraid that he was going to tackle the teacher in the next compartment about my misdeeds, but mercifully he didn't bother.

In Rome we were greatly amused by immense posters all over the city showing Il Duce, with beetling brow and jutting jaw, proudly erecting a signpost marked with the letters SPQR, the abbreviation for 'Senatus Populusque Romanus'. The Senate and the Roman people were theoretically the joint source of sovereign power in the ancient Roman world, even when it had become pure fiction under the emperors. Mussolini, of course, was determined to show that he was restoring the glories of the old Roman Empire.

Some of us mildly disgraced ourselves when we visited a grandiose 'Exhibizione Fascista', and incurred the obvious displeasure of
officials by showing a lack of appropriate decorum and reverence
for the various displays. The teacher in charge of our party
apologised for inflicting this parade of propaganda upon us, but
explained that he had no alternative because the authorities had
cunningly placed in the middle of the exhibition the office where he
was required to have our passports stamped.

However, Mussolini and his fascists are mercifully a thing of the
past. Let us return to the nineties. (But having said that can we really
now be so sure? The outcome of the recent Italian elections, the
emergence of neo-fascists, and, above all, the prominence in the
media of pictures of that glamorous young politician, Mussolini's
grand-daughter, inevitably make me wonder.) So, what about that
undoubted modern menace, the Mafia? Happily, the answer quite
simply is that we saw no evidence at all of their existence, let alone
their activities — with perhaps one tiny exception.

In Sicily, as I have said, we were based in Giardini Naxos. The
Naxos end of this pleasant resort is traditionally the place where the
Greeks first landed in Sicily. There is a minor archaeological site at
this point and a small museum alongside. One afternoon, I thought
that I would go and have a look at this. There were signs indicating
the way along the promenade, but I had difficulty spotting the precise location of the 'museo'. There was an elderly gentleman standing alone gazing out to sea, so I thought I would ask for directions.
My Italian is still, after all these years, pretty rudimentary, but I can
certainly manage 'Excuse me sir, but could you please indicate the
way to the museum?' His response or rather the total lack of it, was
quite extraordinary; he not only failed to make any kind of reply, he
didn't seem to notice my existence, ignored me completely, and just
kept on gazing out to sea. When I mentioned this odd experience
back at the hotel, I was told that this sort of reaction was not at all
unusual in Mafia-dominated Sicily, particularly among old people.
'Hear nothing, see nothing, say nothing', was the long-established
most prudent policy.

However, on the more positive side, we did observe large
notices, prominently displayed in several churches, urging united

resistance to 'La violenza Mafiosa'. These same churches, as I have said, were packed on Sundays with congregations that included a high proportion of young people who sang the hymns *fortissimo* with typical Italian gusto. Perhaps if the Church is now giving a strong lead to these young people, as appears more and more to be the case, there may be hope for better things in the future.

I had looked forward to seeing in Sicily many fine examples of 'The Glory That Was Greece' and I had certainly not been disappointed. However, it was an unexpected thrill when we crossed to the mainland of southern Italy to find in the museum at Reggio di Calabria two superb examples of the art of that amazingly sophisticated civilisation. The Bronzes of Riace, two of the finest works from the fifth century BC, the golden age of Greek sculpture, have only been known since AD 1972, when they were discovered in the sea off the coast of Calabria.

How they came to be there can only be a matter for speculation. The likeliest theory is that they were being transported from Greece to Italy when their ship was wrecked in a storm off the coast of Sicily. After anything up to 2,000 years in the sea, they were obviously in need of extensive cleaning and restoration. When this process was completed, the experts were so impressed by the sheer quality of these two large bronze male figures, each over six feet tall, that they have pronounced them as probably from the same workshop as the famous Elgin Marbles, the sculptures from the Parthenon in Athens, now in the British Museum. Some scholars even maintain that they were probably the work of the master Pheidias himself.

These latest additions to the world's store of ancient Greek masterpieces are naturally given five-star treatment in the 'Museo Nationale' at Reggio di Calabria. The museum was only selected to house this priceless find after fierce competition from the famous galleries of the north of the country. This decision in favour of Reggio apparently was taken as part of a new policy to encourage economic development and tourism in the south, previously notoriously neglected by governments in Rome and big business in Milan.

As another example of this new, enlightened policy, we found that all motorways south of Salerno are now free of tolls. This should come as welcome news to any motorist familiar with the hole in holiday budgets that motorway tolls can make in almost every country of western Europe except Great Britain. What's more, these *autostrade* are a real pleasure to travel along. For mile after mile they are bordered on both sides by beautiful multi-coloured oleanders which seem to make them much more bearable than the usually bleak, dusty equivalents in our country.

It's perhaps worth emphasising that the museum that houses the priceless Bronzes of Riace at Reggio is a 'Museo' *Nationale*. Therefore, as with the Greek temples of the same period over which I enthused in the chapter on Paestum, and their accompanying 'museo', you can make as many visits as you wish free, gratis and for nothing, provided that you are a foreigner over 60 years of age — and have not left your passport back in the hotel.

It's also worth mentioning that we found that everything a tourist needs is far cheaper in the unfashionable south than in the popular tourist cities of the north. For instance, a campari soda, my favourite Italian refreshment, cost me little more than half of what I had paid only the previous year in a square in Florence, and everything else, coffee, tea, postcards, souvenirs, were correspondingly cheaper.

The rest of our tour around the 'heel and toe' of Italy might have been designed to illustrate that old adage 'Half the world doesn't know how the other half lives'. There could not possibly be a greater contrast in domestic arrangements than that between the dazzlingly white conical 'trulli' of Alberobello, a little town in the province of Apulia, and the super-slum troglodyte cave dwellings of Matera in the obscure province of Basilicata. Nor between both of those and the elegant desirable modern residences provided by converted eighteenth century palaces in Lecce in Apulia.

A thousand or so of these 'trulli' make the little town of Alberobello look like nowhere else in Europe. 'Trulli', which are round, beehive shaped dwellings with conical roofs painted in brilliant white, present a quite dazzling spectacle in the bright Italian sunshine. Michelin surpasses himself in Alberobello and says, 'The quarter is all white and seems to have been built for Snow

White and the Seven Dwarfs by oriental magicians'. As you might imagine, camera shutters and Eric's pencils were all working overtime.

The occupants of the 'trulli' shyly and discreetly make capital out of their remarkable residences. We were invited into one by a smiling, welcoming lady to observe how, despite their unusually shaped exteriors, they still contained reasonable mod cons and creature comforts within. The lady resident very gently and agreeably contrived to convey the impression that she would not be offended if we cared to reward her appropriately for her trouble.

A greater contrast could scarcely be imagined between the picturesque 'trulli' of Alberobello and the squalid 'sassi' or cave dwellings in which till 1960 some 15,000 inhabitants of the lower town of Matera existed, all huddled together with their livestock, and with little light and minimal sanitation. The houses and even a few churches were all hewn out of the rock face. Not surprisingly in these wretched conditions, diseases were rampant and life expectation was short. The residents were forcibly removed by the Italian government to modern housing nearby some 30 years ago. Ironically, there is now a purpose-built 'strada panoramica' from which these abandoned slum dwellings in tiers on the hillside can be conveniently viewed and photographed.

Definitely the other extreme of the housing spectrum can be seen at Lecce, a town in Apulia of unexpected beauty and opulence, the well-heeled part, as it were, of the 'heel' of Italy. In the central square, the Piazza St Oronzo, there is a sort of Nelson's column with a statue of the saint on top, surrounded by a group of extremely elegant baroque buildings, all in a lovely yellow limestone, which have caused the town to be dubbed 'The Baroque Florence'.

There are also beautiful seventeenth and eighteenth century buildings grouped around the Piazza del Duomo, of which the most notable is the Church of Santa Croce with a veritable riot of extravagant baroque ornamentation on its façade. Finally there are many eighteenth century 'palazzi', former homes of the rich and noble, which, in the long years of economic depression in the south of Italy, became run-down and neglected. However, the modern entrepreneurs of once again prosperous Lecce are busily buying them up and restoring and converting them into eminently elegant and desirable residences for the 'nouveaux riches'.

From Lecce we drove south to the Capo di Santa Maria di Leuca on the extreme 'heel' of Italy, and regarded rather as the Italian Land's End. At the point where the Ionian Sea meets the Adriatic stands the Church of Santa Maria de Finibus Terrae — St Mary of the Ends of the Earth. There is a cherished tradition that this is the spot where St Peter, the first Pope, first set foot in Italy.

There is another firmly held tradition amongst the southern Italians, said Terry our knowledgeable Saga courier. According to this, one must make a pilgrimage at least once in a lifetime to Santa Maria di Leuca. In return, on arrival at the Pearly Gates on one's final heavenly pilgrimage, St Peter will accord automatic admission. The official local brochure thinks this is obviously reasonable. 'Is not this resort', it says, 'with its brilliant sunshine, its colourful villas, its blue sea, its good works, a real foretaste of Paradise?' We thoroughly agreed.

Villa of Tiberius, Capri

Epilogue

'T is true that a good play needs no epilogue', said Shakespeare in *As You Like It*. Nor, therefore, should a book, whether good, bad or indifferent. However, there are a few loose ends in this one that I feel I need to bring together.

My main problem has been what to leave out. This applied particularly to Part One where, in order to do justice to the pilgrimage to Compostela, I had to reject other areas of Spain that were strong competitors for inclusion. I am now wondering, for instance, how I could possibly have omitted the fascinating province of Castile with its wealth of 'Castles in Spain'. There we were based in the handsome city of Segovia with its fairytale Alcazar, where the great Isabella was crowned queen. The historical significance of that event, plus the impact on English history of her daughter Catherine of Aragon, gave Rosemary food for thought indeed. While for me there was that quite incredibly massive Roman aqueduct, still in good working order after just celebrating its two–thousandth birthday.

Nor can I understand how I could possibly have omitted mention before now of our Spanish teacher friends, Fernando and Maria Nieves de Pablos, who have lent us many times their very attractive chalet on the Costa del Azahar, the Orange Blossom Coast. I was there again last August and the beaches were still astonishingly uncrowded, and the traffic on the nearby motorway still pretty negligible. This area also has attractions for nature lovers, since within easy reach is the vast estuary of the River Ebro, reminiscent of the French Camargue with rare birds such as cattle egrets and pink flamingoes.

With regard to Part Two, I have already mentioned that I have accepted advice that our pre-revolution memories of Poland would now be out of date, while the former Yugoslavia is all too obviously and tragically not a tourist attraction at present. Yugoslavia was the last country that we visited before Rosemary's illness put an end to our many years of happy retirement travel together. It therefore has a special place in my affections. We continue to be haunted by the present unbelievably tragic events in Bosnia.

When we stood on the historic bridge in Sarajevo from which Gabril Princip fired the fatal shot that assassinated the Archduke Ferdinand of Austria and precipitated the First World War, the 'war to end wars', we saw a normal peaceful city around us with a predominance of Moslem mosques and minarets. We could never remotely have imagined that this city would shortly be the centre of another ghastly tragedy. It is equally unbelievable to us that some crazed barbarians should have shelled the sublimely beautiful city of Dubrovnik, in our opinion second only to Venice as the most beautiful city in Europe. Deeply ironic too, since Dubrovnik's unique attractions stem largely from its having survived unscathed all the wars of other centuries down to modern times.

However, there is one part of the former Yugoslavia which perhaps deserves a special mention in this epilogue, namely Lake Bled in Slovenia, which was the place in Yugoslavia that we visited most recently. Purely on the score of natural beauty our English Lakes, such as Wastwater with Great Gable in the background, or Derwentwater with the Jaws of Borrowdale beyond, might stand comparison. Where Bled is supreme is that human hands have contrived to add three focal points which enhance to perfection the beauties of nature. First there is a tiny chapel standing on a miniature islet in the middle of the lake; next, conspicuous at the town end of the lake, is the parish church, with a tall, slender spire in russet and cream. Finally, dominating the whole idyllic scene on a great crag, is a romantic baroque castle.

Slovenia seems to have established its independence with a minimum of trouble, and the new government is assuring potential tourists that the state is perfectly safe. The British Foreign Office appears to agree. So, whenever Saga in its wisdom deems it prudent to restore Lake Bled and its equally spectacular neighbour Lake Bohinj to its brochures, enterprising pensioners might do well to put it high on their shortlist of possible holiday destinations. Yugoslavia was always one of the cheaper holiday countries; with the new Slovenian government desperate to revive its tourist industry, it should be an even better bargain now.

Perhaps some further comment or clarification on Part Two is desirable. The Saga holidays described there were obviously spread over a number of years, and not all of them are now on offer in exactly the same form. However, almost all the places that we visited and which are described in Part Two are available, some as optional excursions, in one holiday or another on offer in the current brochures.

And now my final thought. When I was a child, my family used to travel all of 15 miles to the Fylde coast for our holidays, and a jolly good time we had too. This year friends and relations have taken their holidays in India, Egypt, Florida, the West Indies, the Gambia, Thailand and Kuwait. I know they have all enjoyed themselves as well. However, I'm worried that the seductive convenience of modern air travel may tempt the new pensioners to whom this book is primarily addressed, to think that further is better, and thereby overlook the endless wonders and delights waiting to be discovered and enjoyed by them in almost every corner of the continent of Europe, just across the way.

If the small selection of those wonders and delights described in this book has aroused the interest of some of those pensioners, actual or potential, it will have achieved its purpose.

Notes on Your Holiday